FIERCE
Wholeness

ROBIN MEADE

FIERCE
Wholeness

FINDING MYSELF AFTER
CHILDHOOD EMOTIONAL TRAUMA

Published by Redemption Press, PO Box 427, Enumclaw, WA 98022.

Toll-Free (844) 2REDEEM (273-3336)

Redemption Press is honored to present this title in partnership with the author. The views expressed or implied in this work are those of the author. Redemption Press provides our imprint seal representing design excellence, creative content, and high-quality production.

Scripture quotations marked ESV are taken from the ESV® Bible (The Holy Bible, English Standard Version®), copyright © 2001 by Crossway, a publishing ministry of Good News Publishers. Used by permission. All rights reserved.

Scripture quotations marked MSG are taken from The Message, copyright © 1993, 2002, 2018 by Eugene H. Peterson. Used by permission of NavPress. All rights reserved. Represented by Tyndale House Publishers, Inc.

Scripture quotations marked NIV are taken from the Holy Bible, New International Version®, NIV® Copyright ©1973, 1978, 1984, 2011 by Biblica, Inc.® Used by permission. All rights reserved worldwide.

ISBN 13: 978-1-64645-011-4 (Paperback)
978-1-64645-012-1 (ePub)
978-1-64645-013-8 (Mobi)

Library of Congress Catalog Card Number: 2020902138

Contents

INTRODUCTION

Personal Landscape

I DID NOT THINK MUCH of my story of healing until I started sharing it with others. Being marginalized to the point of having your personhood stolen is a subtle process, much like erosion to a floodplain, a landscape that otherwise would have potential for growth and strength and beauty. Pieces of you erode a little at a time, weakening the structure of your personal landscape, until one day, big chunks of you have washed away.

The women in my mom's family are petite. At five eight, my mom was the tallest. She was a size six when she and my dad married. I took after my father's side of the family. I am tall with broad shoulders, more of a swimmer's build or a linebacker. By the time I was eight, I was five feet tall and had to start wearing a bra. By the time I was eleven, I was six feet tall. Before each growth spurt, my feet would grow a size or two, and I'd put on weight. Then once I grew, everything evened out. Somehow, regardless of my height and build, I was expected to fit into a smaller size. Mom clipped on not just about how fat I was but how my behavior did not measure up and how all these things embarrassed her and our family.

As I grew up, there was an increase in confluence, a steepening of the slope of the floodwater of my mother's anger, magnifying its force of erosion on my sense of self. I had no control over how tall I was or how fast I was growing, but the weight of my mother's unrealistic expectations—flooded regularly by her anger at having unmet expectations—and abrasion, large rocks of gaslighting from my father, as well as boulders of unresolved family conflict carried in the force of the water, pummeled and wore down the land of my sense of self.

Over time gradient, or sideways, erosion assaulted the land of my sense of self because when surreal things happened to me, I could not comprehend them, and I always questioned my reasoning abilities. Lateral erosion occurred as my land succumbed to the lesser waterways of self-doubt, self-flogging, and poor relationship choices. Incongruity between myself and my faith joined the main force of an angry river. I had lost sight of who I was and where I was.

This book is not about dieting or how a diet helped me lose all my excess weight. This book is about my healing journey from the emotional baggage of my childhood created from growing up in a floodplain.

The journey to figuring out and understanding the actual deposition of the river, where it is appropriate or not appropriate for the river to flow, has taken most of my adult life and faith walk. This journey is highly personal. There are some elements in this book that will work for everyone, but the timing for each will differ because each person's circumstance has different needs that may require different responses.

Once I understood where the river should flow and where it

shouldn't, I tried to improve the drainage to reduce the water levels of anger in the land of my sense of self through setting boundaries. Through trial and error, I was able to set healthy boundaries with every relationship in my life. Once I was able to set strict boundaries with my parents, a dam was built that has permanently prevented my land from being uncontrollably flooded. But there was much more work to be done in rebuilding the strength of my personal land.

While building the dam prevented further damage from flooding, internal healing took time and support came from a loving community of other believers. Dealing with forgotten pain, things you stuff down just to survive, is serious business. This pain is so ingrained into your life experience that it affects the feelings you have, the decisions you make, your attitude, your reactions. Some pieces are small and easy to work through. Other pieces are enormous, messy, hairy chunks that are intimidating and exhausting to rebuild.

To rebuild the structure of my personal land, I had to plant Scriptures in my heart, terraces of grass for a strong, solid foundation for my land. With this foundation, I began to internalize who God is and who I am in God's eyes. This led to opportunities to invest in shrubs of self-worth that I could plant to further strengthen my land. I had no idea my land would produce such beautiful shrubs. Now I saw myself more and more through God's eyes than through the paradigm of my upbringing. I was no longer helplessly sitting back being flooded. I decided to step out in faith and plant the trees of my hopes and dreams. God met me where I was, my trees flourished, and now I enjoy the vast beauty of the whole landscape that God and I have created.

My journey is not complete. I am not someone who has "made it," but I have come quite far from where I started. I don't have a quick fix to recommend. I don't have a diet to recommend. This book is about the restoration of sin in my life, about seeing the goodness of God in the land of the living, and about fierce wholeness through hope. What I do recommend is a relationship with Jesus Christ, taking a lot of time and honesty to understand who you are and why and having a supportive group of believers to stand with you. This has made all the difference for me—and I know it can make all the difference for you.

1

Growing Up in the Floodplain

And Jesse made seven of his sons pass before Samuel. And Samuel said to Jesse, "The Lord has not chosen these." Then Samuel said to Jesse, "Are all your sons here?" And he said, "There remains yet the youngest, but behold, he is keeping the sheep." And Samuel said to Jesse, "Send and get him, for we will not sit down till he comes here." And he sent and brought him in.
1 Samuel 16:1–13 ESV

CONSIDER THE STORY OF David's anointing. His father, Jesse, presented all of his brothers first. What does that say about David? Was he an afterthought? Was he considered unimportant or inconsequential in his family? Jesse knew that Samuel wanted to see his sons, but Jesse didn't call David from his shepherding duties until specifically asked.

David was the youngest, and I can relate to David because I am the youngest in my family. I don't know how many years separated David from his next sibling, but nine, thirteen, and fifteen years separate me from my three siblings. Maybe Jesse didn't want to be troubled with finding someone to take over the shepherding for David. Maybe Jesse didn't think that David was important enough to be called to Samuel with his other sons. Surely Samuel would be more interested in one of the older sons. Samuel thought so too, yet God corrected him, reminding him that God sees us differently, looking at the condition of our heart instead of our outward appearance. I wonder if David felt dismissed, unimportant, invisible in this family. I wonder if he also felt the burden of all his untapped abilities, wondering when he would be able to develop them and use them. I know I felt this way for years, always wanting but not understanding how to get there.

I grew up in Grand Rapids, Michigan, the third daughter trailing my last sibling by nine years, the youngest of four children born to the same parents. As the caboose, a surprise, a mistake, my life was an odd combination of being controlled and being neglected. By the time I was eight years old, I had already learned the unwritten house rules: make my mother happy, stay out of trouble, and get along at all costs.

Growing up, I spent a lot of time in my room, although I never felt it was my own, controlled space. Because it wasn't. In 1971, when I was six years old, I had my very own bedroom next to my parents' bedroom; however, my room did not have a door, just a doorway. Anyone could walk into my room at any time. I was not allowed to set boundaries on my room or my person.

I would not get a bedroom door until I was eight, but it was a shutter door, not a solid door. At night I feared the monster eyes staring at me through the shutter and wanted so badly to cover this door, to have real privacy. Still, I was happy to have my own room. At least, I was told I should be happy that I was being given my own room.

In the other corner of my room, I had a gorgeous dollhouse. My mother had always wanted a dollhouse and found a handmade one at an estate sale. The royal-blue dollhouse had white trim, and each windowsill had three plastic roses sticking out of the sill. The front door was white with a gilt doorknob. There were three floors with two rooms on each floor. Each room had its own variety of wallpaper, from pretty grey and blue or pink striped wallpaper with a window painted to overlook the countryside to rich baroque gilt wallpaper with ornate scenes of aristocratic couples dancing. The second-floor room had wallpaper picturing bookshelves filled with books. I suppose this should have been a library or study, but I thought it made a perfect bedroom.

For furniture, I had covered little blocks of wood with fabric in pretty pink flowers on a yellow background using staples, and voila, there would be a new couch. I showed my mom the couch I had made.

"I bought you furniture for your dollhouse," Mom said. "I spent the money your grandfather sent you for Christmas."

What I really had wanted to spend that money on was a Dawn doll because they were the current doll that would actually fit into the dollhouse. "I can make my own furniture," I said, incredulous.

Nevertheless, my mom preferred more traditional furniture that fit the ideal dining room, living room, bedroom, bathroom—both in her house and in my dollhouse. But it was the 1970s. I wanted bean bag chairs and bead curtains.

My mom said, "That 'couch' doesn't really fit in the dollhouse. It looks like a piece of trash. Why are you always so ungrateful? When I was little, I would have given anything to have a dollhouse like this."

Although my mother always won the conversation, I struggled

in my spirit to work around her demands and preferences. At one point I unscrewed the top and used the "attic" for extra things. I was very proud of myself for discovering the attic. After all, it was my dollhouse. I felt I should be able to use some creativity to play with my options.

"What have you done to the dollhouse?" my mother demanded.

"I made some furniture. Everything doesn't fit in the house now. I need storage space. We have storage space in the basement in the furnace room."

"But you've ruined the dollhouse!"

"No, I haven't. Look, the screw goes back in. See how nice the parquet floor is in there? Just like a real attic. I can switch out the furniture and keep everything together in the house. This way none of the furniture will get lost."

My mother frowned but didn't say anything else. "Hmpf" was the last she had to say about it, which either meant she had to retreat and think of a better argument or she didn't think arguing was any longer worth her time. Whichever the case, I had won this round of conversation and the right to store dollhouse furniture in the attic.

My mother had always wanted a canopy bed, so she purchased a bedroom set with a matching bed, dresser, and desk for me. The canopy bed was full size, intended to grow with me, but I would have been content with any bed that fit in my room. I liked the idea of bunk beds so I could have a friend sleep over because all my friends had sleepovers. I thought spending time with friends this way was more important than having a big canopy bed I slept in alone.

The dresser was a lingerie dresser, tall and thin. My play clothes, pajamas, and underclothes were in my dresser, but the rest of my clothes and the clothes of other women in my family were all but packed in my closet. My clothes took up about half of the small closet. My uniform jumpers and Peter Pan–collared blouses were hung up next to my Sunday dresses. I remember having four or five pairs of shoes: Sunday shoes, tennis shoes, school shoes, and boots. I grew fast and so did my feet.

The desk fit very nicely in the corner of my room by the window. The desk had storage on both sides for files or books or whatever I wanted. I was interested in art, crafts, designing clothes, writing, and reading, so I filled the desk with all those things. Since no one showed me how to organize the things I wanted to keep, I shoved everything into the drawer or desk shelf. Once they were stuffed full, it was time to sort through the papers and choose which ones to keep and which ones to throw out. I wanted to keep every paper, so these decisions were hard for me.

My walls were painted yellow, deemed my favorite color, even though I really preferred light blue. My mother strictly guarded how my room was decorated. No ridiculous posters or other youthful expressions were allowed because of the inappropriate culture they projected. I was allowed a knickknack shelf, a painting of a little girl with a teacup, and a bulletin board, all of which my mother had picked out herself without my input. The knickknack shelf had been populated with things my mother had collected and thought should be important to me.

While everything about my bedroom was controlled and chosen for me, the only thing I had complete control over was a daily schedule that I kept on my bulletin board, among the articles, pictures, and letters. For the daily schedule posted on my bulletin board, I preferred thirty-minute increments and was frustrated when I felt forced to use odd time increments. Some tasks took me twenty minutes or thirty-five minutes instead of an even fifteen or thirty minutes. I could do fifteen-minute increments, but if the task needed twenty minutes, I would bristle at the disorder of it all. I would try to better my time to get the task to fit into my schedule. Giving myself more time than I thought I needed for a task would have easily resolved this conundrum, but giving myself more time seemed like losing to me. Cutting time from the tasks made my efforts seem more efficient and more deserving of praise.

This schedule represented the ideal of what I was to do, and the time increments gave me control over how long I had to complete each task.

The effort of making the schedule was tremendous, but following the schedule was haphazard. I made a new schedule at the beginning of each school year, each calendar year, and for each summer vacation. Already at six years of age, I felt an intense need to win approval regardless of what it cost me. This was my first lesson in optics, a reaction to the chaotic emotional environment around me. Employing optics gives the impression that everything is as it should be when it really isn't. For example, I was organized with my schedule, ready to contribute what was necessary and worthwhile, but in actuality I did not follow my schedule. I had shoved all my toys under my bed instead of putting them away, even though I had written "put away toys" on my schedule.

My room was messy, a perfect outward example of the underlying chaos in my family. I could not get in the habit of making my bed or picking up my toys. No one took the time to show me how to clean my room. No one took the time to explain to me how accumulated dust could make you sick. I was expected to know how to clean by observing and to have mastered doing so. I hated cleaning my room because I would always fail at it. When I asked for help, I was told how lazy and ungrateful I was for not wanting to clean such a beautiful room.

My method of cleaning became similar to the way I dealt with my emotions: swept under the bed and out of sight. Everything was still there, just not as tidy and certainly not visible. It wasn't that I didn't want my bed made or my toys picked up. I very badly wanted to want to clean, to have my room look like one of the clean rooms I saw on television. But I always thought, *Why start something I was going to fail at anyway?* The whole idea seemed ridiculous to me. Avoiding the situation by sweeping my things under the bed seemed like a much better idea. This habit of avoiding dealing with the root cause of how I felt and why I felt that way took a firm hold in my life, even at a young age, and began to control the inner me.

Other than creating my daily schedule, the only external aspect I was allowed to control was my time. Outside of playing cards with the family, no one was interested in spending time with me. I played with my dolls, drew all kinds of pictures, and sometimes played with the kids down the street. At age five, I started reading and writing well. I had a set of classics that captured my attention and I spent a great deal of time reading. Although I didn't understand all the content, I knew how to look up words in the dictionary and ask questions.

No one greeted me on the way home from the bus at age six, so I carved out my own path in the afternoons. My first stop would be to visit Mrs. Van, our elderly neighbor, after school if I could not get the key to work or if I forgot my key. Mrs. Van was a very nice lady and seemed happy to listen to me chatter about my day. I remember she made tea for us and always had cookies.

Because I enjoyed reading, I loved to write, and wrote my first fully illustrated book. I was so excited about my accomplishment that I called three New York City publishers who would surely want to publish my book. This was in 1971 when local and long-distance service was all handled by AT&T. I had no idea about phone charges, long-distance charges, or how much my calls cost, and when the phone bill arrived, my parents were furious.

"Robin, what were you thinking?" my mother demanded. "You spent all this money on long-distance calls!"

"I wanted to tell them about my book. They might want to publish it." I was just trying to make things happen. I hadn't known to ask for permission because I only used the telephone daily to call my friends down the street.

"Oh," Mom gasped in frustration, "you cannot use the phone for long-distance calls, ever! Who is going to be interested in a stupid little book that you wrote with all your scribbled pictures? It's not as if the artwork is even passable. You will never make any money with nonsense like this." She waved my book in front of me.

"Robin," my father said more reasonably, "you need to ask permission for long-distance calls. They cost a lot of money. Your mother and I have a budget to manage and to pay bills."

Money was an important source of conflict in our family and with my parents.

I nodded obediently, but went to my room, crying. I felt flustered and anxious. How was I supposed to know about how much things cost and what a budget was? I thought writing a book was an accomplishment. Like my doll-furniture making, my book-writing efforts were falling short of the mark, and I began to think that maybe I would never make it, that all my ideas seemed stupid and worthless no matter how much effort I put into them.

From then on I kept my writing to myself and journaled regularly. Since I was often alone, I had plenty of time. I wrote down how everything felt. I wrote stories. I wrote about how I felt life should be, how I should be. I wrote prayers to God.

2

An Increase in Confluence

*Don't push your way to the front; don't sweet-talk your
way to the top. Put yourself aside, and help others
get ahead. Don't be obsessed with getting your own
advantage. Forget yourselves long enough to lend
a helping hand.*
Philippians 2:3–4 MSG

THERE'S A SAYING THAT goes something like this: Be the woman
who chooses to help another woman straighten her crown instead of pointing out how the crown is lopsided. Certainly, putting
our jealousies and our selfish motivations aside, and focusing on
loving and helping each other is the obvious choice over dishing
out sheer criticism.

But not everyone is at the point in their life where they can
display loving, honorable traits. What is modeled for us as children

becomes normal, but when this modeling opposes what is written in God's Word, then seeing situations from a different perspective becomes necessary for us to question that "normal."

My Oma (Dutch for grandmother) was from the Netherlands, and her children went to high school with my older sisters. She and her husband lived near downtown in a beautiful house with rich wood accents on the inside.

She was kind but firm, and my first glimpse at what a mother should be. She made Dutch-style crepes called *pannenkoeken* for breakfast when I would come to her house first thing in the morning. This was the first time I had seen a woman cook in the kitchen because my father did all the cooking at our house.

Oma was the babysitter I spent time with before I started grade school. She knew how to knit, crochet, do needlepoint, and sew. She modeled patience for me when she taught me, and I was thrilled to learn all I could about these crafts.

Oma operated a side business out of her home as a seamstress. I remember her dining room frequently filled with bridesmaids' dresses displayed on dress forms, waiting for their owners to come and try them on. I was five or six, and would sit on the wooden bench in the dining room bay window while she sewed. We would talk about her technique.

To give me something to do, she taught me how to knit. She told me I should always think of good thoughts while creating something so the person who would own it would be influenced by these thoughts. I remember her praying over the dresses she created.

Armed with this new habit, I would be careful to sit still and think good thoughts while I was creating. This was challenging when I tangled the yarn, but I would patiently sit and work through the knots. This was my first exposure to what God might think about what I was actually doing in the moment.

My parents bought me a sewing machine for Christmas when I was seven. I took sewing lessons and created a few outfits for myself. In practice on my own, I made mostly doll clothes, then I spent a great deal of time watching television and playing with my Barbie dolls or Dawn dolls. My dolls would have fights about who got to date Ken, who had the job that made the most money, and who was dressed the best. The dolls had very dramatic lives and were shocked at hearing the news the other had to bring. These dolls were often one-upping each other. One doll was always prettier, better dressed, or had a man and the other did not have at least one of these things going for her. The doll with this going for her was better than the other doll. The other doll wished she could be like the cool doll.

Once, I ironed one of their polyester dresses trying to get a wrinkle out. The iron was too hot for the fabric and melted a hole right through part of the skirt. It became the "disaster" dress. The doll that wore this dress had just survived a fire or a car accident or being robbed. Ken would always rescue her, they would fall in love, and then she would make Ken a list of things he had to do for her to keep the relationship going.

I hadn't realized it then, but this sort of play acting I did with my dolls mirrored my relationship with my mother.

Time with my mother was more formal than sitting at home playing games or watching television. My mom would have me dress in my best dress and take me to lunch and shopping. In line with the idea of looks trumping reality (optics again), dressing up was my mom's favorite thing to do next to shopping. We needed to look a certain way in order to go shopping so other people would think we measured up with a certain level of society.

Now, I grew quickly and was usually uncomfortable in clothes, especially dress clothes, not to mention I was also tall. I was always uncomfortable, self-conscious, and felt too big to fit into "normal" spaces.

On one particular outing, my mother and I arrived at a restaurant for lunch and walked up to the seating hostess. There was a fancy podium for the seating hostess with a gilt lamp. Though, it was lunch time and in the indoor lighting dim, the sun provided enough light to see. There were small trees with shiny dark-green leaves in the waiting area on either sides of the benches and next to the podium. The other people in line waiting for the hostess were pairs and trios of older ladies and couples. The older ladies were dressed in a similar fashion to my mother and I, on the formal side. The couples did not seem as dressed up, but no one was wearing jeans.

Looking around, I noticed there were no other mothers with daughters my age dressed up, and I wondered why, but I did not ask. Perhaps I was being treated like an adult with all the adults around, which made me feel as if I had "arrived" in that world where I might have some insight into what was really going on around me.

As we waited for the hostess, my mother carefully removed her gloves.

The lace collar on my dress itched terribly, but it was the latest fashion. One of the women in front of us was wearing white shoes, although Easter was a few weeks away. I knew this was poor etiquette and took note of it, waiting to see if my mother had noticed.

But she stood perfectly still, holding her gloves.

"How many in your party?" the young and thin, blond-haired and blue-eyed hostess asked. Her fingernails had a light pink-polish and just the correct amount of makeup that accented her facial features. Her navy-blue, A-line dress matched her navy, low-heeled pumps. She reminded me of a television actress.

"Two," my mother said authoritatively. "I'd like a booth, please."

"Please" for my mother meant "you had better do it this way." I'm not sure why my mother preferred a booth to a table. Maybe she thought the conversation could be more private.

I nodded in agreement, smiling. I'm not certain if she saw me, but I didn't want to miss any of my "adult" social cues.

"Of course," the hostess said, keeping her smile the whole time. "Please follow me this way." She gracefully took two menus and gestured toward the direction of our booth.

We followed her to our booth through the restaurant. I glanced up at the oblong glass ceiling, where the late winter sun shone down on the small trees between the tables. A planter with trees and different-colored flowers sat by the booth area. I wasn't sure if the flowers were real or artificial, and they looked so pretty, it seemed rude to ask.

"Here we are," the hostess said, placing the menus on the table. "I hope you enjoy your lunch."

"Thank you," my mother said evenly, making eye contact with the hostess, then watched her walk away, studying her.

"Thank you," I said quickly, to make sure I covered my etiquette bases.

We removed our coats. I copied my mother in carefully folding mine and placing it in the extra space on my seat in the booth. My mother carefully placed her gloves on top of her coat. I was already sitting straight in my seat with my hands folded on my menu.

My mother sat down and clasped her hands, smiling at me. "Did you see that woman wearing white shoes?" she asked, looking straight at me.

"Yes, I did. Easter is still a few weeks away." I knew this was the appropriate response. I partially held my breath, waiting for my mother to continue.

"Yes," she said, smiling and looking away from me to pick up her menu.

When her gaze was not focused on me, I knew I had gotten the answer at least partially correct. I heaved a small sigh of relief as she continued her critique of the woman we had seen in the lobby.

"I wonder if her husband doesn't make enough for her to be able to afford to buy shoes proper for the season. Now, that hostess is dressed for success. She will land a rich man in no time. She has a perfect figure. Her makeup was perfect too. Why, she could be a star like Elizabeth Taylor, or marry well and leave work behind like Grace Kelly." She said all this without making eye contact with me. She was waiting for me to respond, for *how* I would respond.

"Her shoes match her dress perfectly too," I offered, cowering slightly behind my menu, but peeking over it to watch my mother's response.

"Yes," my mother agreed, but did not look up.

Yeah! That was two answers correct for me. My anxiety slowly subsided. *Lunch may be fun today*, I thought.

"Here you are, ladies," our waitress said, placing a water each in front of us. The waitress smiled broadly at me. I perked, honored to be referred to as a "lady" just like a real-live grownup.

The waitress was close to the same age as the hostess, but she wore the prescribed uniform for the waitstaff: a white blouse, black skirt, and black loafers. She had curly brownish-red hair that seemed to have a will of its own and large brown eyes. Her makeup was limited to eye liner and mascara. She was pretty in a different way than the hostess and seemed more relaxed, more personable. "What would you ladies like to drink?"

"I would like some iced tea," my mother said, "and my daughter would like a glass of milk."

"Mom," I started bravely. This was going well so far, I thought. "Could I have a milkshake?" I loved milkshakes. They were so delicious. The waitress and I both waited for my mother to respond.

"Now, Robbie, if you're going to have a nice figure, you can't be drinking milkshakes for lunch. You're outgrowing that dress fast enough as it is," my mother said sweetly. "What are the specials today, dear?" she asked the waitress.

The subject of the milkshake was now completely closed. I slumped a little in my seat with the itchy lace collar rubbing against the underside of my chin, disappointed that my efforts to please did not warrant a milkshake. Being rewarded with food was already important to me.

"Our soup today is the French onion. The specials are the baked salmon with lemon rice and green beans; chicken piccata with mashed potatoes and steamed broccoli; and the sandwich of the day is the Rueben with French fries or a side salad. Do you have any questions about the menu, or do you need a few minutes?"

"Those all sound very good," my mother said. "Would I be able to order the chicken with the lemon rice instead of the potatoes?"

"I will ask the kitchen and be right back," the waitress said.

"Robbie, do you know what you would like to have for lunch?" my mother asked me as soon as the waitress was gone.

"I would like the Rueben with fries, I think," I answered, adding the necessary room for my mother to correct my choice. She would choose with or without the "I think" from me, but that made me feel as if I was giving her the option instead of her dictating my choice.

"Reubens are always so tasty," my mother said. "Are you sure you want fries with it instead of a salad?"

The question was clearly a trap. What kind of stupid question is that? Who wants a salad instead of fries? How ridiculous.

"Yes," I said, mustering all the confidence I could, "I am sure I would prefer the fries." The failed attempt at the milkshake made me question what I would actually be having for lunch.

Our waitress returned then. "Ma'am, we can certainly substitute the lemon rice for the mashed potatoes with the chicken."

"Oh good. I'll have the chicken with the rice then. Robin, go ahead and order."

"I would like to have the Rueben with fries, please," I said in my best adult manner.

The waitress wrote down the order and gave me a quick smile. My mother didn't look at her at all, but glared at me the whole time.

"Very good," the waitress said. "I'll take your menus. Your food will be right out." And the waitress left to do her job.

"I bet the hostess is going to college, or maybe has graduated already and is looking for a husband. I wonder if our waitress is going to college." My mother commented, maybe to herself.

I answered her anyway. "The waitress seems very nice."

"Nice, yes," my mother began, "but she will not be able to land a doctor or a lawyer like the hostess. She doesn't have the same style or grace"—my mother sighed, shaking her head—"and she is a little fat. Robbie, you do understand how to act properly so you will have opportunities in this world? You have to dress correctly for the occasion, be able to discuss current events or talk about classic literature. You've already started reading the Greek myths and legends. This is a wonderful start."

I nodded. "Thank you."

"Thank you" seemed a neutral response, and I couldn't go wrong with a neutral response.

My mother felt I should be well spoken, wellread, educated, beautiful, and thin. "Mom, what if the hostess or the waitress don't fall in love with any of the men who are doctors or lawyers? Who will they marry then?" I really wanted to know because I knew not all men were in those professions, and they had wives and children.

"This is one of the opportunities I was just speaking about, Robin," my mother answered curtly. She said this as if I should know what she was talking about, but I didn't. And she called me Robin instead of Robbie, signaling that she was now annoyed with me.

I felt as if surviving this lunch would the same as climbing a sand dune while fighting giant scorpions with a butter knife. My anxiety rose, and I chewed on my fingernails. "Aren't the flowers pretty?" I asked, trying to change the subject. At this point, I had a fifty-fifty chance. "There are so many different colors."

"I think they are all fake," my mother responded, crushing my hope. "It would cost a fortune to have so many real flowers in bloom this time of year."

"I got my report card yesterday," I said, trying again at more positive conversation. "I got Very Satisfactory in every subject but gym. In gym, I got Satisfactory." In grade school, Very Satisfactory was the best you could do. Usually my grades or what I was reading were shoo-ins for turning the conversation around.

"Oh, Robbie, that's wonderful." My mother beamed.

Bingo! One scorpion down.

"Don't worry about gym class. The other classes are what matter. People who are good at gym class brag about it because they are too dumb to read or think for themselves." My mother is very intelligent but was never athletic.

But I didn't agree with that statement. Some of the girls in my class at Catholic school were good at sports and academics. But I didn't want to argue with my mother because we hadn't gotten our food yet.

"I'm almost done reading *War and Peace*," I said. *War and Peace* by Leo Tolstoy was quite thick and filled with inappropriate themes for a child, but my mother felt the book was a classic, so inappropriate themes didn't seem to matter to her. She told all her friends I was reading the book, but I didn't care for the story myself. The plot lines in the novel seemed too emotional to me.

I remember wondering why anyone would have sex with someone who wasn't their spouse, or have to get permission to marry the person they love, or think of the leader of the opposing side in a war a hero? But my father said that nothing was really that bad.

"What do you think about the story so far?" my mother asked, genuinely looking forward to the discussion.

Scorpion two down! I had to play this game with her, as it was the only way she would love me and spend time with me.

"I don't know what to think of Napoleon," I said. "He seems like a jerk." I'm sure my mother would have preferred a more polished response, but I was just a kid.

"He was a jerk," my mother answered. "Russia at the time of Catherine the Great was a very powerful nation."

"Here you are, ladies," our waitress said, arriving with our food. She placed my mother's chicken piccata with rice in front of her and my Rueben with fries in front of me. "And here is some ketchup for your fries. Is there anything else I can get for you?"

"No," said my mother, considering her plate.

"No, thank you," I added, putting my napkin in my lap. I was hungry, but the conversation made me anxious, and eating was the tool I had in my toolbox to reduce anxiety.

My Rueben had beautifully marbled corned beef thickly piled on it with fresh sauerkraut and Swiss cheese melted to perfection. There was even extra Thousand Island dressing on the side. The French fries were thick cut and deep fried to crispiness and hot. I wasted no time eating my sandwich. In less than five minutes, the Rueben was gone. I took a little more time with the fries.

My mother was not a slow eater, but she took more time than I did. "Wobin, did woo wike ur rooban?" My mother usually talked straight through a meal while she was eating.

I twirled a fry in some ketchup. "The Rueben was very good." I mean, it certainly looked good. I ate it so fast, I barely tasted it. I had learned that getting to do something was more important than actually enjoying it. Like most food for me, eating the sandwich quickly soothed my anxiety.

When my mother finished eating, I still had a few French fries on my plate. I was mostly full.

"Robin, you need to finish your food," my mother said.

I bristled internally at this comment because I knew later while shopping for clothes, she would comment about how fat I was. The two directives did not align, but I silently finished my fries as directed.

The waitress returned. "How was everything?" she asked. Our plates were both completely empty except for the garnish.

"The chicken was very tasty," my mother answered.

"My Rueben was yummy," I answered, trying to keep up.

"Wonderful," the waitress said. "Will there be any dessert for you today?"

"Oh no," my mother said, smiling at the waitress. "Dessert is for those who have salad for lunch. I'll take the check." And there it was. The last scorpion pinched me in the back just as I had neared the top of the sand dune. Game over.

"I'll be right back with the check," the waitress said, smiling and nodding at my mother.

"Since we're trying on clothes, you don't need the dessert," my mother said to me, looking me straight in the eyes.

In my head, I was screaming, *Yes, I know. I got it the first time* because I couldn't say this out loud. I simply nodded, and my shoulders slumped. The good grades and reading novels did not really matter. All that mattered was what my mother wanted right then and this was for me to be thin. Even though I did learn some valuable information about how to properly present myself in society, these lessons were learned at a great cost to my body image.

3

Abrasion

*Keeping steadfast love for thousands, forgiving iniquity
and transgression and sin, but who will by no means
clear the guilty, visiting the iniquity of the fathers on the
children and the children's children, to the third and
the fourth generation.*
Exodus 34:7 ESV

My mom was the oldest of three daughters born to Slovak immigrants who had come to Chicago. My grandfather worked for the railroad. My grandmother could functionally speak English after being in America for three weeks. That's about all I know about her. My grandmother passed away from complications from toxemia a couple weeks after giving birth to my mother's youngest sister.

My mother and her sisters went first to their aunt and uncle's house to live so their father could continue working. My mother's aunt was nineteen. She had a six-month-old daughter of her own to care for. Now she had two toddlers and an infant as well. This was during the Great Depression, and while immigrants had opportunity, they also had hardship. My mom and her sisters were passed around to family members and their godparents until my grandfather remarried.

My grandfather remarried a woman who had little tolerance for his existing children. My mother was still a young girl, smart and tenacious in a world with little tolerance for either intelligence or tenacity from her. Her stepmother favored her own children most, berated my mother, and physically abused her.

My mom ran away to live with her aunt and uncle when she was thirteen. This situation was left unchecked in my mother's family. When I was growing up, I remember my mother, her stepmother, stepsister, and sisters always fighting. Always fighting. People in her family would fall in and out of favor with my mother. My mother had a falling out with her cousin because my sisters were not chosen to be in her cousin's wedding as flower girls. My step-aunt was harsh toward my brother, so we no longer saw her or spoke to her. Additionally, my mother did not care for one of her brothers-in-law, so we did not visit that aunt. This varied depending on the year.

My siblings will recall different memories of being around the people I did not interact with at all. We were all expected to side with my mother even though we had no idea what the fight was about. My mother was right in everything, and the other person or people were wrong. There would be no discussion of any possibilities outside of her conclusion.

My mother married my father and moved to Michigan, but she could not leave Chicago behind. She used her tenacity to focus on bitterness. She had expectations of her family and demanded that these expectations be met. Often her expectations were not met.

An example of her expectations going unmet happened when I was expecting my son in my early thirties. This was in 1998, nearly fifty years after my parents had married and moved to Michigan. My mother wanted to have a reception at my house in Brookfield for some of her second cousins. Their parents had taken my mother in for a time when she was a child and then again as a teenager. These cousins lived in Iowa and were in contact with my mom, but not the rest of her siblings.

I prepared my famous chicken salad, baked cookies, and pulled out my beautiful pink china to prepare for whoever would attend. I knocked myself out to make the occasion nice for my mom. I knew this was important to her.

But my family and my parents and these second cousins were the only attendees.

"I can't believe it. I'm going to call them again." My mother was furious. My mother's siblings had not said they weren't coming. This was the fifth or sixth time she was calling to leave a message for each of her sisters. "I just don't know what could be more important than coming to see family from out of town."

I was worn out from all the effort of entertaining by the end of the day. The cousins had left, and my mother was still complaining about who did not show up.

"Mom," I said, frustrated, "aren't you happy *you* got to see these cousins? I really knocked myself out for this to make it nice for you. Aren't you at least thankful that I made this effort for you?"

"Yes, yes, everything was very nice, Robin. That is not the point. Ruth and Bessy should have made the effort to come. Gloria and Steve, well, they don't like this side of the family because they helped me when my stepmother was so cruel to me."

The reality was that no one else said they would be there. They just didn't come. An invitation from my mother meant you were committed to coming—not your response to the invitation, just the invitation itself. They had responded with "we'll see" and "maybe" because they had learned over time that saying a flat-out no to my mother would only end in a huge fight.

All the rest of us listened to the ranting for hours, days, months, years. My mom confused what she wanted to happen, her expectations, with what everyone should do. This isn't unique to my mom because most of us do this. But the difference with my mom is that her behavior escalated over the years because no one was willing to set boundaries with her. My mother's tenacity could have been harnessed for great things for God, but this was not her choice.

My father grew up in a family where he was favored as the youngest of two children and the only son. His mother had lost her only brother to appendicitis as a child, so she treated my father as "the prince." There was a lot of criticism in his family, and my father learned from his father to not make waves. My father married a woman much like his mother.

My father loved my mother very much and would do anything for her. While he was alive, my mother felt he was beneath her. He did not have any emotional boundaries with my mother, and she continually belittled him. Only after his death did she realize the depth of his love for her.

My father kept the peace in our house by dismissing the hurtful things my mom would say. Some of the gaslighting phrases he would use included "She didn't mean that," "You're all right," "Don't worry about it. Just move on," and "Your mother just wants what is best for you." For years I blamed my mother for everything without considering the part my father played, and the price he asked his children to pay just to keep peace in the house.

My father taught me how to add by teaching me cribbage. The rule "according to Hoyle," as my father would say, was that the other player could claim uncounted points. I was five when I started playing cribbage and was very motivated to keep all of my points, so I learned this math quickly.

I played cribbage with my dad almost every day of my childhood. We would talk about things in general. I would ask questions. My dad would answer what he knew, and the great thing about my dad was there was no judgment about anything. He would entertain any question or proposal for action with simple critical-thinking questions. We would discuss potential outcomes. He would steer the conversation in the right direction, but he rarely expressed anger or disappointment in my questions or topics.

My mom, however, did not play cribbage. Cribbage was "your dad's game." As a family we would play Canasta on a Saturday night or Sunday after church. My brother, who was nine years older than I, had a horrible temper and would often throw huge fits of anger if he was losing. In a card game with my sister once, my brother screamed at her, called her a bitch, and flipped the card table over because he was losing. My father let him walk off without consequence. My sister vowed never to play cards with him again. The game was left unfinished and we all retired to watch television, help with the dishes, or take a walk outside.

My brother was an equally insufferable winner, rubbing in his victories without end. His temper, like my mother's, was tolerated by my father. In my mother's eyes, my brother, her only son, could do no wrong. She would attribute his behavior to something "upsetting him," his job, his health, or even something disagreeing with him from supper.

Our home was far from spiritual, but we attended church every Sunday. We attended a Lutheran church because this was the Christian denomination in which my mother was raised.

"Your father was raised in the Christian Reformed Church," my mother would say. "Christian Deformed, really. He agreed to go to the Lutheran church because that's *my* church."

The Lutheran church was the only church as far as my mother was concerned. I don't remember the services too much, but I remember the dresses that I wore as a little girl in the summertime with my white summer shoes. I felt adorable in these dresses. I remember looking at flowers and for bugs and snakes in the church yard after church.

By the time I was in school, both of my parents were teachers in the local school system. Even though we were Lutheran, I attended a private Catholic school. The theology differences confused me a bit and started my conversations with God. All the tradition seemed fine, but what did it really mean? If we weren't supposed to have any gods before God, wasn't praying to Mary wrong? My mother encouraged me to read about Martin Luther. Then I had to know if the Ninety-five Theses was still a thing. If we were all Christian, why didn't we all go to church together? No one could give me any clear answers.

I asked for a pastor to come and answer my questions. He was able to answer some of them, but referred me to books I could read. I attended Sunday school, and memorized the books of the Bible and the Apostle's Creed and the liturgy of choice for Sunday morning at the Lutheran church we attended.

I received my first communion at age ten. My Catholic classmates had been receiving communion since first and second grade. I received it at school too even though I hadn't officially been allowed at the Lutheran church. I did not know how to explain the differences to my classmates. They were all doing church the way they knew how. I just wanted to fit in and not be asked more questions. They all knew I wasn't Catholic. Receiving communion didn't seem like that big of a deal. I said nothing and was hugely relieved when I was official at my home church. I had no idea which way was right, and I very much needed to know what was right because I didn't want to go to hell.

When I was seven or eight, we started attending a Lutheran church on the wealthier side of town. My mom made extra fuss about my Sunday dresses and etiquette while attending this church.

Not long after this, my oldest sister had an encounter in her twenties with the "born again" movement. She invited my dad to come with her to a service. He did and shortly after he got saved. My father started having devotions faithfully every morning. For many years, my mother was unmoved by this. "Holy rollers" was the term she used to describe my father and sister. The Lutheran way involved reciting the liturgy, not reading the actual Bible that the liturgy was based upon.

Though my parents claimed to be believers, "Children obey your parents" in Ephesians 6:1 was certainly quoted to me quite often, but "Fathers, do not exasperate your children" in Ephesians 6:4 was totally skipped. Our church was not focused on discipleship or accountability. Not to say that there weren't some true believers in attendance—I'm sure there were—but holding people accountable in their faith walk was not part of the package at our church.

My mom was more concerned about optics, about us looking like the family who "had it all together" and went to church together every Sunday. Perhaps this supported her illusion that our family was meeting some set of expectations she had in her head about families.

Even though we went to church every Sunday as this happy little family, it was anything but happy at home. Family gatherings usually involved a huge fight between my mom and someone else. I don't remember a single enjoyable holiday or family gathering that was peaceful and loving. Preparation for the holiday or gathering would start days in advance, with my mother and father planning the meal and calling the guests to make sure they knew what time to arrive. Whether or not they would arrive was never questioned. If my mom called and told you what time to arrive, you were expected at that time.

Most holiday gatherings would involve just our immediate family. This was in the 1970s. I was in grade school, my sisters were in their twenties, and my brother in his late teens. (If I was ten, my brother was nineteen, and my sisters twenty-three and twenty-five.)

Baking was my mom's area, although she did not do so often. If she baked for the occasion, this would be done the night before. My father would negotiate that he needed the kitchen to himself the day of to prepare the main meal. The night before the occasion, I would help my mother set the table.

My mother carefully considered all the china in the cupboard. "I just don't know if I should use the Christmas China or my Slovak blue china." She wasn't asking for my opinion. She was just talking out loud to herself. "Robin, someday when you are married to a doctor and have a home of your own, you will have the Slovak blue china. The pattern is so unique. You'll be the only one serving on it for special social gatherings." Now she was talking to me.

China was a status symbol to her. Having several sets was thrilling, a sign of her own "arrival" to a desired level of social status with other accomplished people.

I had learned that there was nothing correct I could say about being bequeathed the china. I usually just nodded and asked my next question. "Should I use the plates and the bowls for the salad?"

"Use the bowls," my mother would direct. "We aren't having soup today."

I started pulling the china plates and bowls out of the cupboard. They were kept in a storage area where no one went for anything else to protect them from potential damage from day-to-day interaction.

"Remember, Robin, there needs to be a fork for salad, a fork for dinner, and a fork for dessert at each place. Everyone needs two spoons—one for dinner and one for coffee." My mother would repeat this two or three times to make sure I got it.

"Ok, Mom," I said, nodding, although she was in the kitchen and couldn't see me. I saw helping as an opportunity to show myself as a contributing member of the family team. Plus my parents were doers, so helping was modeled for me. "Which napkins do you want to use?"

"Use the white napkins with the lace on the edges," she called from the kitchen. "And give everyone a water glass and one of the crystal wine glasses. You may also have a wine glass."

My father had already put the extra piece in the middle of the dining room table to make it long enough for everyone. My mother had already put a beige plastic tablecloth under her delicate lace tablecloth. In the middle was a centerpiece of crimson poinsettias appropriate for the occasion.

The day of the gathering there would be a lot of tension around cooking the meal and having the table just right. My mom was overwhelmed by cooking meals in general, so my father usually cooked dinners for holidays and company. My dad was a great cook. His roasts and gravy were legendary. My mother would be in their bedroom fussing over some details with presents or decorations or her own appearance for most of the day of before anyone arrived.

Guests arriving would be photographed immediately upon walking in the door. When the doorbell rang, my mother would come out of her room with her camera and start clicking. The pictures proved to whomever my mom wanted to impress upon that her children or important guests were visiting, and to show we were a happy, normal family.

"Merry Christmas!" my mother exclaimed. *Click, click, click* went the camera.

My sisters, Ruth and Diane, arrived at the same time. "Merry Christmas, Mom," my sister Ruth said. "Hang on, let me take off my coat. Where would you like our coats?"

"Oh, I'll hang it in the closet," my mother answered. *Click, click, click* went the camera.

"I've got it," Ruth said. She hung up their coats in the front closet right by the front door.

"Merry Christmas, Mom," my oldest sister, Diane, said, hugging my mom. "The tree looks so nice."

Our real Christmas tree was decorated with all the heirloom ornaments that my mother treasured and had collected over the years. Garland and bright lights wove in between the ornaments for a truly joyous sight. Under and around the tree were presents wrapped in the Sunday comics and reused wrapping paper from past Christmases.

"Oh, you look so slender in that color, Diane," my mother said.

Diane was always dressed appropriately and acted appropriately. We were all expected to dress appropriately for these dinners.

"Thanks, Mom. You look nice too," Diane answered, smiling.

"Here, everybody, come and take a picture in front of the Christmas tree," my mother directed. "Gregg, Robin, come to the living room for picture." She called to us, trying to get everyone in front of the tree. Maybe deep inside she knew this was the only opportunity for a family picture. "Oh, Gregg, I wish you would have worn a nicer shirt."

"I'm wearing what I'm wearing," Gregg retorted. "Take the picture." My brother was the only one who would speak this way to my mother, and she would let it slide almost every time.

"Robbie, get in front," my mother said, moving on. *Click, click, click* went the camera. "Stay there, everyone. Let me get another." She would get at least two, maybe three. "Oh, I'm so glad all of my children are home for Christmas," my mother beamed.

Once the hullabaloo of the arrivals was over and pictures were taken, we would all sit at our assigned seats at the table. The timing of these family occasions was when dinner was ready to be served, and there was rarely any visiting before eating.

"Let's say grace," my father said. He prayed over the meal, thanking God for it, and for all of us children and for our safety and growth over the past few months or year.

After the "Amen," my father would say, "Dig in," or something like that.

Eating was a tricky business at the holiday or special occasion table. "Would anyone like beets?" my mother would ask. "Robin, would you like beets?"

"No, thank you. I don't care for beets."

"Well, I love them," she would quickly say, as if my not caring for them somehow negated the validity for her to enjoy them. "Gregg, would you like some beets?"

"No," my brother would say firmly. "I've told you many times I don't like beets. Why do you keep asking me?"

"Pass them around," she would say. "There are other people at the table besides you."

No one other than my mother liked beets. The dish of beets would go around the table untouched and end up carefully placed near my mother's plate. The same scenario would be repeated for cranberries and sweet potatoes. My mother would ask everyone no less than five times to try the beets and the cranberries and the sweet potatoes. All these dishes would go around the table again each time, coming to their final resting place by my mother's plate.

Occasionally on the third or fourth go around, my father would take a spoonful of each to cover himself for any later discussion with my mother. After dinner my mother would comment, wondering why there was so much of the beets, cranberries, and sweet potatoes left over.

I'm not sure why, but my mother would steer the conversation to whatever she wanted to discuss with one of us that we did not want to discuss. This was usually a choice one of us made about our lives that my mother disagreed with. This is what would start the fight. Maybe the happiness of the occasion was too much for her to process. Maybe she felt with all the happiness, this was perfect timing for her to get her way. A typical discussion at the table would start something like this.

"Ruth, how is work?" my mother asked. This wasn't always the topic, but this is the way the fight would start.

"Work is fine."

"Fine" was normally an acceptable, neutral word.

"Have you considered going back to college and getting your degree so you could get a better job that pays more money?" My mother's answer to everything was to go to college and get a degree so you could get a better job. She and my father were brought up in the era of doing so. That's how they both ended up with careers in teaching and belonging to the very strong teacher's union during the 1960s and 1970s.

There is certainly nothing wrong with a college degree, pursuing a college degree, or encouraging your children to go to college. However, there are certainly other ways of making a living and goals for employment other than making the most money ever.

"No," my sister answered flatly. "I like what I do." My sister made enough money at a decent job she had worked at for several years. Her goals were to work to support herself, but also get married and be a mom. Different goals than going to college and becoming a doctor or a professor, but legitimate adult goals, nonetheless.

"Diane went to college and really enjoys teaching," my mother countered in a tone that displayed shock at Ruth's defiance. "You could do that too."

"I'm not Diane," Ruth said with a little agitation in her voice. She understandably did not appreciate being compared again. "I'm not interested in going back to school."

"But you could get a better job that pays more money."

Ruth kept chewing, obviously agitated at this same old discussion happening again. For years this discussion happened at several of the family gatherings during the year. This time the discussion was with this sister, but it would also happen with my brother. Neither of them had college degrees.

"How are the Vikings looking this season, Gregg?" my father interjected. This was usually my father's best effort at deflecting. As the head of the family he could have said, "Let's not talk about this today," or "Let's talk about something else," or "Please shut your pie hole and stop upsetting everyone." But he said none of these things. And so my mother would continue, unchecked.

"Robin, you should have some more salad," my mother said, passing the salad toward me. Whoever she passed it to would obediently continue passing the salad bowl to me. I would take a couple tongs full of salad. And mashed potatoes and meat and gravy. Salad tastes better with mashed potatoes, meat, and gravy. I ate quickly, stemming my anxiety with the amount of food I could shove into my mouth at once. I was not old enough to leave the house and go anywhere, so I would usually listen while my soul was ripped to shreds at my mother's satisfaction.

"Better football season than the Lions," my brother said with a big belly laugh. My dad loved the Detroit Lions as only a loyal fan could. My brother loved the Minnesota Vikings.

"Ruth, you should enroll next term," my mother said, undeterred by my father's effort at levity. "If you are making enough, you can afford it. Why wouldn't you want to better yourself?"

"I'm not having this same conversation with you again, Mom! I don't want to go back to school. It's not for me! Please drop it!"

"Well," my mother continued, "I don't know why you're so upset. There's nothing wrong with me suggesting that you have a better education. Your father went back to school. I went back to school. You only attended one term. How could you possibly know?"

At this point there would be some expletives and tears from my sister, and she would leave the table, leave the house, leave the family gathering.

Once she had left the house, my mother repeated, "There's nothing wrong with my suggestion. An education is a good thing for everyone." No one commented to the contrary and so she would feel her position was justified. Dinner after the fight was finished mostly in silence. There was always a closing comment to me from my mother along the lines of, "Robin, you really need to watch what you are eating," or "Robin, why didn't you finish all your food?" or "Robin, you ate quite a bit."

I always felt trapped at this point. I wasn't on my own and wasn't old enough to be on my own, but I felt like somehow I should be better, more independent, more able to meet my mother's expectations. This conditioning in my home life is what made me vulnerable to other unhealthy relationships in adulthood. I didn't know there was a different, healthier way of relating.

After dinner my father would suggest a game of canasta to get everyone focused on something else. Usually my mother would not join the game, choosing to retire to watch television in the other room and be by herself. There would be no resolution to the conversation. No apologies. No effort to restore the damage done to any of the relationships in our family.

4

Gradient Erosion

You hem me in, behind and before,
and lay your hand upon me.
Psalm 139:5

SOMETIME BETWEEN THE AGES of nine and twelve, or maybe for the whole time, my parents had a crisis in their marriage. I remember thinking if they divorced, processing through who would be best to live with, or how I could run away and make it living on my own. Maybe I would live in the woods like the Swiss Family Robinson, or live off the land like the Ingalls from *Little House on the Prairie*. I had watched the television shows. Compared to the life I was living right now, living off the land didn't seem that difficult.

My parents went to a Marriage Encounter retreat that changed their relationship dynamic permanently. My father may have considered divorce, but with his newfound faith and the influence of the retreat, he was committed to make the marriage work. After this retreat, my mom was willing to have morning devotions with my father. We continued to attend the Lutheran church on the wealthy side of town.

In the middle of this time, one Sunday upon arriving at church, I decided to sit next to some of the widow ladies. They all sat together in some pews near the middle section of the church on the left side of the sanctuary.

"Dad, can we sit here? I think they would like to sit next to a family instead of sitting alone."

"Sure," my dad said.

But my mother insisted on sitting in the back of the church, always. She had "female" issues, always. She made a big deal about the stress of her female issues and how she needed to be close to the bathroom. She did not sit with us and the widow ladies.

This is how we met Marie. Marie was a wonderful, kind widow lady with no children of her own. She and my father started a friendship because they were both interested in business, real estate, investing, and playing cards. We started sitting with Marie every Sunday. Then we started going out for brunch with Marie after church.

After a few months, we started going to Marie's house for dinner. Then my parents would leave me at Marie's house and go on trips for the weekend. Over time, we started taking trips with Marie to different parts of Michigan. I so enjoyed being with Marie because my mother's behavior was much less volatile around her. She still lost her temper, but she was checked somehow by Marie just being present.

Marie was a true Southern woman from Kentucky, a sharp dresser with proper etiquette and presence. She knew how to manage money and had done well for herself in the market. My mother is very smart, but she has never had a head for business. My mother was jealous of the friendship my father and Marie had.

On the weekends or evenings when I would stay with Marie, we would do things. She encouraged me in my crafting. She did not sew or knit or crochet, but she thought that I did was amazing. Over and over she would say, "That's so beautiful what you made" or "How talented you are!" These words were such a balm to my already deeply damaged young heart, but I did not believe the words. Yet I knew there was hope they were true because Marie was so good to me in everything else she did. Marie was kind but firm, just like my Oma. She loved to cook and taught me how. We made sautéed mushrooms and rich sausage gravy. She showed me how to make pie crust from scratch. She loved me and invested her time and love into me. This was such a change from the life I knew.

Marie was also strong and independent, not unlike the women in my family. She had been on her own after her husband died, but even before then, she was strong and independent. Like me, she was on the tall side, five-ten, so she understood my struggles with being tall. She was intelligent and tenacious but with a grace that my mother did not have.

Marie had good boundary-setting skills and self-discipline. She did not lose her temper over spilled milk or messy plaster of Paris models made for science projects. Things did not have to be perfect for her. She was able to think and keep herself composed even when she was frustrated or angry. She would think through situations and we would discuss the possibilities logically. She modeled these skills for me.

Thank goodness for the friendship with Marie from church. I was able to spend time with her when my parents needed a sitter.

When I was nine, my brother, then eighteen, tried to rape me. My craft things and dolls and dollhouse had all been moved to the basement near my brother's bedroom. I spent a lot of time in the basement playing, crafting, and watching television. My brother was already addicted to pornography. I wasn't inappropriately dressed. I wasn't behaving inappropriately. I was an available victim. I managed to kick my brother and run upstairs. I immediately told my parents. My father took action to make sure I was not in the house alone or the basement with my brother again because up until this point, my brother had often been my babysitter.

My mother, however, dismissed the incident altogether. She simply refused to acknowledge anything of the sort had taken place. My position of value in the household became inescapably clear to me. I was worth nothing.

Because of the situation with my shutter door, I hated the lack of privacy in my bedroom, and rearranged my room over and over to give me the most privacy, to keep anyone from watching me through the shutter. I was convinced my brother was doing so. Sometimes I could hear him breathing on the other side of the door.

The layout of my bedroom would change in what I could change, but I could never arrange the furniture to block the full view of the door with the canopy bed.

So one day I took apart the canopy bed. I moved my bookshelves perpendicular to the doorway and put my mattress and box spring behind it to give me complete privacy.

"What have you done to your bed?" my mother demanded.

"I took it apart," I answered. "I want my room this way."

"You don't want the canopy bed? Do you know how much that canopy bed cost? When I was a little girl, I would have loved to have had a canopy bed. You are so ungrateful."

I would take apart the canopy bed three more times before my mother relented and let me have just the twin bed. My canopy bed was given to my niece, a little girl who would appreciate it. But my twin bed was just enough room for me, just as the schedule I had created and posted on my bulletin board was just enough time for me. These were the boundaries for myself.

My walls were still strictly guarded. I could not change the shelf, but I could change the contents with things I had picked out myself and paid for with my own money when we went on trips to Amish country or the Upper Peninsula or at church camp. The painting of the little girl with a teacup was now above my new twin bed. I could not change the picture, but I could change its location.

I was defiant enough to make incremental changes, as long as I complied to my mother's standard of excellence on the outside. She didn't care what was on the inside.

5

Lateral Erosion

*How precious to me are your thoughts, O God! How vast
is the sum of them! If I would count them, they are more
than the sand. I awake, and I am still with you.*
Psalm 139:17–18

WE MOVED TO THE wealthy side of town before my sophomore year of high school. My father and Marie wanted our
families to merge into one house. Our family had been friends with
Marie for about five years at this point, and she was now in her
late seventies. She did not have any children or any family nearby.
Marie was financially able to purchase the house but did not want
to live alone.

Already, she had had one bout with breast cancer in the middle
of the five years and was in remission. Her chances of the cancer
recurring were high, although I did not know this at the time. My

parents would have never been able to purchase a home in this location on their own. They were still living mostly paycheck to paycheck. My mother's displeasure at my father's friendship with Marie was overridden by the excitement to be moving to an area that would give her a higher social status. She would have been excited by the financial implications if she had had an understanding of finance. She talked endlessly on the phone to all of her relatives, friends, acquaintances, anyone who would listen really, of how her address would now be in "East Grand Rapids." She would emphasize the "East" when giving people our new address.

My bedroom at the new house was quite different. Only my parents, Marie, and I moved to this house. My brother had married his first wife and moved away. I was in the basement across from a large space with our ping pong table and some other random furniture. I had my own half bath that was next to the rather large laundry room. I no longer wanted my childhood desk, so my mom put it in the laundry room to use as her desk. My bedroom was twice the size of my bedroom in the old house. There was a fireplace and enough room for all of my things and all of my crafting supplies. Having the fireplace made me feel very cosmopolitan. I could listen to my records on my record player without disturbing anyone. I had a twin bed. There was even room for an extra twin bed so I could have a friend overnight.

The picture of the girl with the teacup and the knickknack shelf were hung appropriately in their place. I was able to hang an additional shelf acquired on a trip to Europe. Things on the wall still had to meet my mother's approval to be hung. There were no "gaudy" posters of my favorite bands or anything from my school because such things were for peasants and other uncultured folk. Only what my mother considered "classic" and "stylish" could be displayed on my wall. I loved my room anyway. Best of all, I had a solid door that I could close and lock.

For high school, I left the private school world to attend a public high school for gifted and talented students. The curriculum was based off of the classical learning model from Greek society. Mostly I remember writing papers and thoroughly enjoying meeting and discussing life with other smart people. In Montessori through eighth grade, I had attended the same school with the same classmates. High school was a brand-new world for me, but my self-talk was at an all-time low.

I had three close friends in my first two years of high school—Todd, Sarah, and Taj. Todd was the first person I met on my first day. He was a sophomore; I was a freshman. Like me, Todd arrived at school too early. Todd had never met a stranger in his entire life though, so we started a conversation that has lasted almost forty years. Sarah, who sat next to me in my history class, was petite, smart, beautiful, and funny—all the things I wanted to be. Taj was so sharp and very much herself all the time, which was also what I wanted to be. While I talked to Todd every morning before school, I talked to Sarah and Taj every night after school. They were different from me, but they accepted me just as I was. I had never experienced this before at home or at school. It was so refreshing to have people just like me and accept me. I really didn't know how to process this. I wanted to be a real person just like them when I grew up.

There were forty kids in our class year. I had a 4.0, but because my last name started with a V, and the grade point average list was logically alphabetical, I was not in the top three in the class. Had my last name started with an A, my 4.0 would have been nearer to the top. This killed me. My only source of worth at home was my grade point average. This was the absolute only thing I had going for me with my mom. Then in my sophomore year, four events took place that tested me and would set the course for my reactions going forward into my adult life.

The first event was receiving a B my first term in Geometry. I was devastated. Not only was my grade point average completely ruined, the blow came from math, one of my best subjects. There was nothing I could do to win. Kicking myself all the way home,

I prepared myself to face my parents. The ability to hide the grade from them had never occurred to me. Because my parents worked in the school district and knew some of my teachers, I was convinced they would know about my every move no matter what I did. Honesty and forthrightness seemed my best defense. But oddly enough, my mother did not react to the grade as I had anticipated. I was expecting at the very least a lecture on how I needed to pay attention or I was going to ruin my life. Maybe she did not worry about the grade because math was not her best subject. Maybe something she considered more pressing had more of her attention. In any case, perfectionism was so ingrained in me by this point that I was able to self-flog myself into line. And I did a great job.

The formation of this tie, a lifelong view of myself, was the second event that shaped my path into adulthood. This was also the fall that I started dieting in earnest. I was always hungry because I was growing. Then I kept eating after I was done growing. High school. Overweight. Disaster. (I look back at pictures of myself in high school. I was not really fat, I simply needed regular exercise, part of self-discipline I had not developed.) I couldn't rescue my grade point average, but maybe being vigilant with calorie counting would help. I lost thirty pounds from counting calories and eating lettuce and kiwi, probably screwed up my metabolism, and could fit into a bikini. My mother was so proud of me now, as I was tall and curvy, but the style was for girls to wear boy's jeans—Levi's 501 red-tag, straight-leg jeans to be exact. My measurements after my weight loss were 41–29–38. I was six feet tall with beautiful long, wavy honey-colored hair. But all I could see was fat and my crappy 3.91 grade point average. I had thoroughly tied my poor body image to every level of success in my life.

The third event in high school that shaped my adulthood was my faith. Going to church and volunteering and attending youth group comprised the extent of my faith, even though I went to catechism class and was confirmed. To me, catechism seemed like an awful lot of effort to make commitment to God official. I just wanted a "right" way to be. My life was so chaotic. I wanted to end the chaos. If I could just know which way to go, I would go. During catechism class, we were all saying what we needed to say to be confirmed because our parents expected it of us. I started to question what God was all about. My faith wasn't really going anywhere. The catechism lessons seemed to talk about more than just memorizing and repeating phrases. I thought the lessons were talking about a God I could interact with as a person. But I didn't see this modeled anywhere, so I didn't know how to "get there." I wanted to be wherever "there" was, and I talked to God but didn't feel I had a relationship with Him.

The most devastating and fourth event in my sophomore year was when my mother was the English literature teacher at my school. My mother was in a battle for her position with the overall county school administration and the teacher's union negotiated to have her relocated to the position available which matched her skills and experience. The principal at our school was unhappy with the placement being forced upon her school, which made my mother understandably nervous. Suffering herself from a lack of self-worth made her level of nervous pretty high to begin with, but with the additional pressure, she buckled in front of the strong intelligent students at my school. Not one of my peers had a single positive comment to make about my mom or her teaching.

"That's *your* mom? She's a horrible teacher."

"Your mom is an idiot. She's been wasting over half of class taking attendance."

"I like English class. I'd actually like to be learning something instead of listening to her mispronouncing the same names every single day."

Walking down the hall or in the cafeteria, I had trouble making eye contact with anyone. I sank down into my seat. I wasn't suicidal, but I really wanted to die, and I wanted everything to go away. This coping mechanism is what I had learned from my father and his codependency. If the situation can be easily resolved by you doing something, do. If the situation is scary, then try to avoid it, ignore it, or run away from it.

My mother lasted only a few weeks at my school. Over thirty students placed formal complaints with the principal. My mother was fired, and the union moved her to another position at another school. I felt so much embarrassment and shame from the whole situation. I felt as if irreparable damage had been done. My mother's fiasco at teaching ensured I would never be accepted again by any of my peers. Certainly all of the whispers in the hallway I heard now were about me and how I must also be a loser because my mother was a loser.

At the beginning of my junior year, I was extremely focused on how much weight I had lost and what great clothes I could now fit into, but what I really wanted was to get away from the aftermath that my mother had left behind. My friends were all involved in other things—Sarah's family had moved away, so she was no longer attending City High. Todd was a senior and preoccupied with senior things. Taj was class president, and started focusing more on theatre—so when the opportunity came to run from all of this, it seemed the best thing to do.

In science, I was required to take chemistry. The small school I attended did not have the facilities to accommodate a separate chemistry lab, so I attended the mainstream public high school up the street. The kids from this high school were not concerned about weighty social issues or engaged in political debates at lunch time. They could do this because the amount of homework at this school was minimal.

"Hey, Robin, are you going to the dance this Friday after the hockey game?" Eric asked. Eric attended Central and was in my chemistry class. He was cute and played hockey.

"She's not going to the hockey game," Mike retorted. "She's going to the football game." Mike and his brother, Bill, played football.

"She's not going to either of your games," Carol said, making an "Oh please!" face. "We are going to the dance." Carol took my arm as she said this like her plan was a done deal.

"Jeff asked me to the football game, so I'm going with him," I said. "I'll see you all at the dance later."

"Ooh, girl!" Carol said. "I'll see you at the dance with Jeff. But we've got to go to the mall on Saturday so you can tell me *everything*."

I laughed because I didn't think there would be much of *everything* to tell, but I was happy to go to the mall.

Life seemed easier for them, and I wanted an easier life.

At City High, we were required to have internships in our junior and senior years in order to graduate. The internship was like a regular class where we spent that hour at the business location working on a project for the business. I wanted to learn about business and was assigned an internship at a small company down the street from the school. The owner explained the project to me, but I didn't understand what needed to be done.

"Robin, for your internship project, I need you to take this list of customers," Mr. Smith said, pulling out a two-inch typed list and placing it on his desk in front of me. He was an average middle-aged businessman with a balding head, bifocals, and a slight paunch under his old bluish grey dress shirt and navy tie. He continued to rummage around the papers and files on his very messy desk. "Oh, and probably this one too." He looked at a second, slightly smaller list and placed it on top of the first one. "You'll take these two lists and work on finding discrepancies."

This was the fall of 1981. Windows was not available. Computers were not widely used yet, and if you wanted to use one, you had to program it to do what you wanted. But this company was an all-paper house. Paper printouts, paper files, paper, paper, paper.

"Okay," I said nervously, overwhelmed by the request. "What discrepancies am I looking for?" I asked, trying to process the information.

"Discrepancies. You know, differences," he said, staring at me through his glasses like I was an idiot.

"Yes, I understand what discrepancies means." I answered, trying to affirm myself. "I don't understand what specific discrepancies you mean. Am I comparing the two lists to find the discrepancies?" I thought we were speaking the same language. I'm sure he did too. I did not have the communication skills or experience to delve into this situation.

"Yes, do that. If you understand what discrepancies means, you should get to work on the project," he answered with finality.

"Thank you, sir. I'll get to work on the project." I picked the lists up off of his desk and heading out of his office. I didn't say anything else, but I couldn't hide my face. I was confused about what I needed to accomplish with this project. I was also defeated about the internship. In my whole short life, I had wanted to be in business, but the reality of business as I had experienced it was a total bust.

As I tried my best to proceed, I asked for clarification on the discrepancies I found, but Mr. Smith was too busy to answer any questions. I remember him talking about "these kids" and their lack of fortitude. I didn't understand how I could accomplish anything without more direction. The tasks he asked of me were not intuitive. I needed this grade to pass, to graduate. I mustered all my courage to ask the principal if there was another option for an internship. I was told "no" rather flatly. I felt as if the principal's dislike for my mother was transferred to me, but in reality, this company was the only option available for an internship in business.

This was the last straw for me. I ran to the regular public high school as quickly as my legs would carry me, and mid-term, I transferred to Central High School. Overnight I became fourth in a class of almost five hundred with my crappy 3.9 grade point average, and did not have to work as hard to maintain it. I could graduate early because I did not have an internship requirement. Everything seemed better with this fresh start.

At sixteen, I was allowed to make all these decisions by my parents. I presented my reasoning and they followed through on their part and signed the appropriate forms for me to turn into the offices at both schools. Maybe since my mother had been fired from my school, she no longer cared if I attended there. I'm not sure if they thought my reasoning was sound or didn't care as long as I was not in trouble. Just as I had been left to watch television and play with my dolls on my own, I was left to my own devices to do what I thought was best. But this was more important than playing with dolls. I had done so much work in the first two years of high school that I needed only a few more credits to graduate. My plan was to complete these credits and to attend junior college during what would have been my senior year. The junior college—called community college now—was just down the street from my new high school. From the other direction, it was also down the street from my old high school. I would be still be able to see my friends from both schools. All I could think about was being on my own. In charge of my own destiny. Going to college while still living at home meant I would have an associate's degree sooner than my peers. This made me better somehow and more prepared for life ahead. This would pave the way for me being able to move out of my parents' house with a solid accomplishment. This was my plan.

But it was not in my plan for what would happen to my dear friend, Marie. All through high school, Marie was in and out of the hospital. There were so many things that I wanted to share with her, but I didn't want to bother her because she was so sick. I didn't understand the inevitability of her condition. In the back of my mind, if I didn't believe something would happen, somehow I thought it shouldn't. I had no idea until she was almost gone that she would be leaving.

I went to see her in the hospital not long before she passed away. I walked in the room. There were tubes everywhere and she looked so weak. But she smiled when she saw me. That smile contained so much determination and fortitude, as if she could get up and walk out of that hospital room any time she wanted. But she couldn't.

"Robin," she gasped, "I am so happy to see you." Her voice was weaker but the same. The same beautiful tone when she always spoke to me, gracious and loving.

"I am so happy to see you!" I said, fighting back my tears. I didn't want her to see that I had lost any hope. She was being so brave, and so would I. "I start college classes in another three weeks."

"Oh . . .," she struggled, "that is wonderful. You are so smart. You will do so well in college." Her eyes opened and closed. Talking to me was taking every bit of strength she had. She loved me so much.

"I miss our canasta games," I said. "I hope you will be home soon so we can play a game."

"Yes." She smiled. "I look forward to that too." This was the sweetest lie she could have given me, to selflessly give me hope. "Make sure you finish school. Be everything you can be."

"You'll be out of the hospital then," I said. "You'll see me graduate." The statement was ridiculous and we both knew it, but she still smiled.

She would indeed be out of the hospital. Right at the beginning of my senior year when I began attending community college as planned, Marie died, which was not part of my plan. I did not know how to grieve her loss, so I stuffed it down as deep as I could. She was certainly a gift from God. I did not have a meaningful relationship with either of my parents. Marie, the person I was closest to, was gone. After her death I wanted to leave the house more than ever, but I wasn't ready or old enough to be on my own. The stress of this reality later caused me to become emotionally scattered and reckless, especially vulnerable to unhealthy ways of relating to men.

6

Comprehending the Actual Deposition

And David said to the men who stood by him, "What
shall be done for the man who kills this Philistine
and takes away the reproach from Israel? For who is
this uncircumcised Philistine, that he should defy the
armies of the living God?"
1 Samuel 17:26 ESV

THIS IS MY FAVORITE verse in the Bible. David, a young man full of faith, talks about this impossible obstacle with all the sass because Goliath defies God. David understands his position in relationship to God as well as Goliath's. There is no question in David's mind about Goliath's fate. The situation is already a done deal.

Wow, what faith. I've always wanted faith like this, but I had no idea how to cultivate this kind of faith. I thought maybe once

I accepted Christ as Savior, there would be a magic wand, or some poof of fairy dust and I would be everything I could be. I knew there had to be more to walking with God than salvation. Like David's journey to becoming king, my faith journey would be long and would require a lot of work. I went to church most Sundays and read my Bible and prayed sometimes. None of this was radically changing my life. I was too accustomed to the habits that accompany lifelong church going. I could play Christian with the best of them, and did not really get serious about God until after college.

This is when I met the first of three men I would be involved with, have a child with, and fight with. As I took the bus to City to Central to take chemistry, Kevin took the bus from his high school to Central to take physics. I had the same teacher for calculus. My class was before physics and there was lunch in between. This is how I met Kevin. He was tall, handsome with blond hair, had gentle blue eyes, gentlemanly and funny.

I was a tornado of emotions when I met Kevin. I would have already been a mess without Marie's death, but that made me more emotionally messy. Kevin was kind and wanted to help me with how I felt about my mom and my life. We spent most of senior year hanging out a few days a week and sometimes on the weekends. I tried what had been modeled for me to solidify a relationship with Kevin: coy behavior, sex, trying to feign interest in what he was interested in, lies about my life to make myself more interesting to land Kevin. Everything but just being myself, which I couldn't do because deep down I felt worthless.

Kevin did not react the same way my father did to my mother when she used these tools. He was not codependent or easily manipulated, which frustrated me. I didn't feel like my efforts were gaining the traction I expected. I misunderstood his kindness for a genuine interest in me. Kevin liked me but he saw the crazy emotional rollercoaster I was riding and gave me a wide berth, and wisely so. He couldn't articulate what was wrong with me, or why he wasn't interested in a relationship with me.

Kevin planned to join the Marines to pay for college and wanted to go to Ohio State. Because of my high school grades, I had a small scholarship to attend any Big Ten school. My father hoped I would go to his alma mater, Michigan State University. My mother let me know she and my father would make it a point to come visit me at Michigan State every weekend.

So I followed Kevin to Ohio State. Kevin went to bootcamp and then straight to work for his dad and then straight into the next session at Ohio State in March. I graduated from junior college with my Associates in May and made my way down to Columbus to start my bachelor's with the June summer session at Ohio State.

When I moved away to go to college, I basically stopped attending church. Everyone was exploring who they were and deciding what they wanted to believe in. Though I didn't stop believing in God, I wasn't interested in really pursuing a relationship with him. There was no one I had to impress at the church I occasionally attended. The service seemed routine and meaningless, and I thought there had to be a better reason to attend church. There were so many different aspects of life coming at me at the same time, and although I had every freedom to choose, this was all the privilege I had wanted, but I also felt the weight of the responsibility of choosing. And I was absolutely terrified of making wrong decisions.

My parents' first visit was during Christmas my second year there.

Within the first fifteen minutes, my mother began rearranging my things in the living room.

"How were your classes last semester?" She picked up one of my knickknacks, a little china doll with delicate features, and moved it from the coffee table to the fireplace mantle. She then moved a knickknack from the mantle and to the side table.

"Good," I said, following behind and putting the china doll back where it was originally. "I had some trouble with all the terms in marketing class, but I pulled off a B."

"Is that because you are working? Did you have enough time to study?" She rearranged some other knickknacks.

"No, I don't think so," I answered, again putting the pieces back. "I have plenty of time to study on the weekends." The deal I had with my father was that he would pay for a class the first time I had to take it. College being what it was for me, I took a full-time job working in the kitchen at a five-star restaurant.

We continued discussing my semester and moving around the knickknacks for about fifteen more minutes. My mother turned to see all her changes had been changed back and said nothing. I was surprised I had won that easily, but accepted my win and carried on with the visit.

Kevin had tried to break up with me when I got down to Columbus, but I would not accept that my will was not being followed. We maintained a friends-with-benefits relationship for most of college. During the winter quarter my junior year, I was pregnant. I didn't get pregnant on purpose, but thought we could work things out, but Kevin's condition was if I had an abortion. I had the abortion, then Kevin distanced himself. My emotional tornado returned but I buried it deep beneath the surface.

The last couple quarters of school before graduation, I had started working at a telecom company that also had an office in Chicago. Because I had always dreamed of being in business, Chicago seemed like the perfect place to take my degree and make something of myself. There was an opening for a customer service representative in the Chicago office with the company I worked for. I applied, got the job, and transferred from the Columbus headquarters to the sales office in Chicago. Kevin and a couple of my friends helped me move to an apartment in Oak Park. Living in Oak Park provided me a reasonable commute to the office in Rosemont.

Even though I moved to Chicago, I could not and would not

let go of Kevin. He lived in Columbus, but we kept in touch. I often traveled back to Columbus with my new job, and within a year of moving to Chicago, I was pregnant again. This time I refused to have an abortion. I didn't know what an atonement baby was then, but I certainly felt it. This was my chance to make all things right with this child, to atone for my abortion.

Kevin had just asked another woman to marry him. I was now on my own, and this was the first time I was willing to turn to God because I needed something bigger than myself for help.

I called my oldest sister because I knew she had a strong faith. Diane had been a Christian for years, ever since she asked my dad to go to church with her. She knew who God was, and He was real to her. Diane seemed to have the relationship with God, the something more that I felt was missing from catechism lessons. She was as close as I could get to actually touching God. My sister prayed with me, and I accepted Jesus as my Savior.

This was the beginning of change for me. Everything did not turn around to my liking because I accepted Christ. I had to raise my daughter alone. But I didn't have a strong support network for my faith. I started attending church, but the location was far away. This made fellowship during the week hard. Only one of the friends in my immediate circle was a Christian, but as far as going through the hard work of putting on the "new man" and putting off the "old man," I was on my own. I struggled to read my Bible and to understand I needed to change. I was still young in my faith, still striving for my own way instead of trying to discern God's way.

In my network of friends, there was a man named David I had met who was interested in marrying me. He was from Canada, had a good job, and wanted to settle down. Things felt romantic around him, but I was not attracted to him and certainly didn't love him. Like Kevin, David was kind. Unlike Kevin, David lived in a fantasy world that could only be maintained in fantasy. My mother thought David was "perfect" for me, as he was well spoken and talked a good game in front of my mother. He persisted in asking me to marry him and listened to my struggles with being a single mother.

David was pagan and not interested in my faith, but was willing to tolerate my Christian beliefs and create a home that welcomed both of our belief systems. He was willing to fill in the gap for me and my daughter. I figured if my mother liked him and he was willing to be a good dad to Joey, that was probably the best I could hope for, being tainted goods myself. I married him when my Joey was two. Within six months of our marriage, the reality caught up with the fantasy, and David left to be with another woman. I was a few months pregnant with our daughter, my second child, Juliann, and would now be on my own with two children.

Why hadn't I asserted myself in my faith? At home, this rarely turned out the way I planned. I wish I had one dramatic incident to illustrate the pivotal point in my giving up on being who I dreamed of being. I lost the hope of being successful as an independent adult, and saw salvation as something that would help me when I was dead, not as a renewal process of my life while I was alive. Sure, I knew there were things that God expected of me as a believer. But I thought maybe God was like my mother, and nothing I did would be good enough. Maybe I needed to be something worthy first and then I could really have a relationship with Him. I mean, I kept sinning, so what use was salvation to me in this life? I would try my best in my own strength to do what I understood God expected of me, but I wasn't healing. I wasn't growing.

During the third trimester of my pregnancy with my daughter, Juli, I was diagnosed with mononucleosis. Joey was three. I had to quit working earlier in my pregnancy than I expected. Money was tight. My husband was gone. My job was gone. I couldn't manage work, and I was faced with the thought of moving into my parents' house.

My days consisted of sleeping, using the bathroom, then taking a nap, getting the mail, and then taking a nap, talking to someone on the phone, and then taking a nap. I stayed in Chicago until after Juli was born because all of the medical arrangements for the birth had been set up there. Just after she was born, I received divorce papers from David. Ten days after Juli was born, I moved my little family to my parents' house in East Grand Rapids, Michigan.

My parents paid for the U-Haul. They drove back and forth to Chicago. Now I was living with them and eating their food. My mother was angry about all the money this cost and told me I needed to get a job as soon as possible. Juli was two weeks old, and I was still recovering from mono. I found a job in a call center downtown and started the next week.

I met a young woman, Julie, my first day at the new job. She was dating none other than my friend, Todd, from high school. I had not spoken to Todd since moving away to attend Ohio State. Todd's mother did not live too far from my parents. He was dating Julie and had a two-year-old daughter from a previous relationship. I had a baby and a three-year-old by two different fathers. We were both in our late twenties and neither of us had grown in our careers according to our master plans. But we were both new believers. I may have been stuck living with my parents, but at least I had someone to really talk to. Todd and I picked up our discussions from high school as if no time had passed. Todd could relate to my faith walk, my disappointments with my career, and single parenting.

At the suggestion of my sister-in-law and to the horrification of my mother, I decided to try out the First Assembly of God on the south side of Grand Rapids. My sister knew I was looking for a more Bible-based church to attend and knew some strong Christians who attended there. My mother referred to this church as the "holy roller" church. She didn't understand why I wasn't happy just attending their Lutheran church. "They all do business together at that church," she said. "Maybe you'll be able to find a husband there."

Juli was three weeks old, I was still legally married, and had just moved from another state. Regardless, getting a husband was what my mother thought was the most important goal for me.

First Assembly of God was just what I needed. The church was huge but had small groups. There was a lot of structure as part of discipleship, healthy teaching, and loving people. My small group met twice a month just a few blocks from my parents' house. I got to see real people living out their faith walks in marriage and in parenting. I spent a year in their membership classes learning what was required of my faith.

During that year, I was baptized. My small group leader watched my girls so I could take the plunge. He and his wife were so supportive of me. I can see it now, but at the time, I didn't understand my emotional damage or their deep love for me. I made friends with other single mothers from the church.

First Assembly had an enormous nursery with the requirement that each parent serve once a month for each service their kids were using the nursery. I loved going to morning service, but I started serving in the nursery as a teacher for the morning service. This was the way I felt called to serve. Because I served in the morning service, I came back for church on Sunday evening. I read my Bible, asked questions, and started listening to praise music and teaching on the radio.

I did faith with these people for five years. I was really growing in my faith there. But I wanted to be married more than I wanted God. It wasn't just my mother's constant droning about finding a husband, but I still thought being married was the thing I had to focus on in life, and what was best for my daughters. Around the five-year mark and when my divorce from David was finalized, I met my second husband, Rick.

I was still so vulnerable emotionally that I didn't see my second husband was a hot mess. My "hot mess-o-meter" was not in service, had never been activated. I thought everything was possible no matter what, that this man was sent from God. After all, who else would want me? Rick was attentive, kind, supportive, good with my girls, interested in building my costuming business, and attracted to me, even though I was overweight.

I was a single mother in my early thirties with two children by two different men, barely making it working at a bank and living with my parents.

He was recently divorced and looking to start over. We could talk about issues and were aligned politically and (I thought) spiritually. We had similar family issues with drama and anger. Rick told me he had accepted Christ as Savior, and although he did listen to country music, I could overlook that.

After three months of dating, we got married. He found a decent job in Chicago and off the four of us went to start a new life as a family.

I repeated the same patterns of behavior with Rick as I had in my previous relationships because I did not know a different way. I focused on my new relationship and stopped spending enough time in the Word to effect real change in my life and did not see what change needed to happen for me to not be vulnerable to volatile relationships.

But when Rick left me, I was broken enough to try God's way in earnest.

7

Improving Drainage

*For people will be lovers of self, lovers of money, proud,
arrogant, abusive, disobedient to their parents, ungrateful,
unholy, heartless, unappeasable, slanderous, without
self-control, brutal, not loving good, treacherous, reckless,
swollen with conceit, lovers of pleasure rather than lovers
of God, having the appearance of godliness, but denying its
power. Avoid such people. For among them are those who
creep into households and capture weak women, burdened
with sins and led astray by various passions, always learning
and never able to arrive at a knowledge of the truth.*
2 Timothy 3:2–7 ESV

THESE VERSES HOLD THE truth of my situation regarding my
second husband. I was vulnerable emotionally, financially,
and spiritually. I was weak because my faith was not strong enough
yet. I was getting there but I had a long way to go. And my defini-

tion of success was having a husband, not having God at the center of my life. I was blinded by this desire, and when Rick and I met, I couldn't see the unhealthy signs of relating: half-truths, issues with his ex, the length of time since he had seen his daughter, the lack of support from his family, and a focus on appearance over substance (a form of optics). I had not given the relationship enough time before getting married.

When we had been married four years and the fighting was nonstop, Rick and I tried to go to marriage counseling. Our pastor asked us to memorize a couple verses of Scripture before we returned. Neither of us understood why. We soon realized that the counseling rested on our memorizing these verses, but the purpose of this exercise was never explained to us, so we never memorized the verses.

My husband had been angry that I discovered he had been unfaithful to me throughout our marriage and had relationships with several women online, grooming them for his next soft-landing place, keeping his options open.

My heart was broken because I loved my husband. There were a lot of issues in our marriage, but the primary issue was codependency with an angry narcissist. I didn't even know this was the issue then and didn't understand how unlikely it was that he would change.

I had confused wishing with hoping and hadn't recognized narcissism for what it truly is because this had always been my "normal." I had grown up with and was comfortable with these behaviors and interactions. But because I didn't want to be like my mother, I modeled myself after my dad, yet didn't recognize codependency for what it is. I didn't understand that my dad had enabled my mother's narcissism and gaslighted the four of us into doing the same. "It's not that bad," "let's play a game," and "you're okay" were all statements I would hear my dad say to me over and over again. He just wanted to "keep the peace," to keep the powder keg from exploding.

Playing a game had always distracted me, but the unresolved situation *was* that bad, and I was not *okay*. My dad's effort to prevent problems had cost me my childhood and my sense of worth. I chose to date and marry narcissists and fell right in step with being the enabler.

As a child I really did not understand the completely different world outside my house. Everything in my house was normal for me. Every child I knew had parents who got angry with them. I didn't see how my family was different, only that my mom was a force to be reckoned with. Like the force of a river current relentlessly wearing away the land on its banks, my sense of self had eroded over time.

Even so, I believed I could be more self-sufficient and deal with any situation. I could press myself a little more, pull myself up by my bootstraps. I didn't want to be rude and demanding like my mom. I was willing to expect more of myself, but not of other people. There's truth and unhealthiness about both these points of reasoning.

Rick complained that my costuming business was in the house. He said that things would be better between us if I got an office for the sewing. So I found an office close by. Moving my sewing business did not help our relationship, but having an office helped my sewing business because I was more productive and working away from the chaos of our relationship gave me new perspective.

As I worked, I listened to praise music and Scripture. This improvement in what I was feeding my mind improved the condition of my heart. I didn't realize how deeply this new habit would shape my future. Much of the praise music contained lyrics from Scripture, messages about my identity in Christ, God's enduring faithfulness, walking by faith and not sight, and trusting God to come through.

In the spring of 2001, I was in a Bible study called The Walk of Repentance with some ladies at church. The study challenged my thinking. Up until this point, my faith was okay, but not transformative. The lessons in the study made me really think about where I was with God. I began to examine and deal with my attitudes on different levels. I read my first *Boundaries* book by Henry Cloud and John Townsend and learned how to set boundaries with my husband.

But Rick did not respect my boundaries. He only became angrier, and I was afraid of losing him.

Even though I could see that the situation was not healthy for the kids, I could not see that it was equally unhealthy for me. Because my sense of worth was inextricably tied to my ability to maintain my marriage, and unless I was tied to a man, I had no standing in society—and this was my second marriage. If I lost this husband, what would other people at church think of me? What would my family think of me? What little hope I had left drained out of me. Within a few weeks of setting boundaries, my husband asked for a divorce after a huge fight over whether I was paying enough attention to him while he was playing video games and talking to his friend on the phone.

I went back to my pastor for counseling. Between counseling and the Bible study, I was able to get my spiritual feet under me. And because I didn't have any steady income, I borrowed money from my parents to help me fund fabric for the coming Renaissance fair costuming season and money from my friends for an attorney to represent me. I didn't really understand all the ins and outs of the court system and needed an attorney to make sure child support was well handled and to protect us in general financially. (I know some Christian counselors would advise against involving the courts, but this move was spot-on for me. We did not have any property or money to fight over, but the divorce process had been dragged out to cost me as much as possible, to break me. Dealing with a narcissist is unpredictable. There is no clear logic to the turn of events. Without representation, I would not have been able to navigate these waters.)

During the marriage, my husband and I had agreed his career

would take precedence while the kids were young. Because my income was sporadic and my credit score was weak, I wasn't sure I would be able to find another apartment. Our current lease was up shortly after the school year ended. I had already been looking for a new place to live before my husband had told me he was leaving. We were talking to a couple who owned a townhouse and would be gone for a few years on a work assignment.

These people were very nice. I had both their boys in class while substitute teaching, and the boys had given their parents rave reviews about me. We met to discuss the lease and the timing for moving in. While we were there, the husband pointed out some furniture stored in the basement. Being a generous man, he offered to let us use it while they were out of town.

When we were leaving the townhouse and out of the couple's earshot, Rick said, "Well, now I know I'll be all set with furniture in my new place."

My stomach sank. He clearly intended to take whatever he wanted to get his end set up. These kind people would never get their furniture back, so I could not sign the lease in good conscience. This situation seemed like a train wreck waiting to happen—and I did not see a way off the train, but just prayed for a way out. My pastor and the ladies from Bible study were praying for me too.

The answer to our prayers came the next day. I was throwing some garbage out in the dumpster behind my office building and saw a lady across the street pounding a "For Rent" sign in the front yard of some townhouses. Wasting no time, I walked over there to speak with her.

"Excuse me," I said, knocking on the screen door.

The landlady came to the door. "Yes? Can I help you?" She was tall and thin with dark hair and seemed to have a reasonable, straightforward manner.

I introduced myself. "I noticed you just put a 'For Rent' sign out front. My husband and I are getting a divorce. I'm looking for a place for me and my three kids. We're hoping to move by the end of June. Could you tell me about this place?"

"Nice to meet you. My name is Susan. My husband, Mike, and I own this building. The current tenant is just about moved out."

My heart soared at the possibility of being able to rent this place that was so close to everything my kids and I needed.

But then Susan said they had to paint, and her husband would have to approve of the application, and they'd need to run a credit check. "I do have another interested party, but that's not final," she said.

My hopes started to crumble, but I said, "I'll tell you up front that my credit is crap, but I'll make sure I pay the rent on time. I am happy to take care of the painting."

I waited for her to say, "No thanks," but she said, "C'mon in" and opened the screen door. "I'll show you around."

The townhouse was perfect, with three bedrooms, a bath and a half, a kitchen with a separate dining room, a living room, and a large open area in the basement separate from the laundry area. There was no air conditioning, but there were beautiful hardwood floors and a ton of space. The location was near the commuter train, near the main bus line, across from my sewing office, and within walking distance the main downtown strip, the elementary school, the junior high school, and the high school. The rent was very reasonable for the space and the location. I filled out the application right there and gave it to her. When I went to back to my office building, I noticed she removed the "For Rent" sign from the front yard.

This was the first time I had ever seen God work like this. Other people experienced these miracles, not me—and I called everyone I knew to tell them about God coming through. I was so relieved to have a path forward, yet overwhelmed by everything that had to be done in only a few short weeks.

As soon as school was out, my parents decided to take the girls on a summer trip across the US to see Dad's sister in Seattle, and then to Alaska to visit my niece and her husband. The girls were nine and twelve that summer, old enough to really enjoy the trip. My son was three, too little to go, so he stayed with me. My dad wanted to remove them from what he anticipated (rightly) to be a contentious situation. Although my dad would not stand up to my mom to correct her behavior, he did recognize the behavior for what it was and would do his best to mitigate the effects in extreme situations like this.

My husband stated he would take care of his own living arrangements. I found a bunch of free, once-used U-Haul boxes and packed the house, arranged for all the utilities at the new house with no issues, and asked our friends for moving and cleaning help.

Moving day came and I was an emotional wreck. My husband had started the day angry and full of sarcasm. I was trying to finish up last-minute details, keep my newfound boundaries intact, and not feel like a marriage failure all at the same time. The situation was overwhelming for me. I prayed, but my prayer was more like a halfhearted "Please oh please oh please," and then I was distracted by what had to be done.

"Everyone is on their way?" my husband asked.

"Yes," I said, "they should be here in about thirty minutes or so."

"I noticed you haven't packed any of my things."

"No, but there are plenty of boxes and tape for you to use to pack them. I've taken care of the rest of the house."

Then I got a call from my new landlady. I couldn't move into the townhouse that day. Immediately I called my girlfriend—her husband was on his way to help—and they had a five-car garage that was partially empty.

"They are doing grout work on the main bathroom and she doesn't want me to move in this weekend. We have to be out of this place by tomorrow. May Nathan and I come and stay with you until Thursday? Then I'll get moved into the new place."

"Just you and Nathan?" she asked.

"Yes."

"Sure, we have room in the garage for your stuff. You and Nathan can stay here. But we can't help you move on Thursday. We'll be working."

"No problem. I'll figure that part out. Thank you so much!" I hung up.

My husband pinned me with anger. "You and Nathan are going to Tom and Ghita's? Where am I supposed to go? You've left me homeless."

Surreal. I felt my emotions turning with the sideways rush of the situation. I tried to focus on directing three-year-old Nathan until everyone arrived, which thankfully was not much longer after this.

When my friends came, they helped move everything and separated Rick and I to keep things moving, which was something I could not do.

Rick was angry that he had to pack, angry that he couldn't just slide into my townhouse and still live with me, angry about who knows what else, and plain angry on top of that.

With my belongings moved into my friend's garage, Nathan and I settled into their guest room for a few days. A huge weight had lifted, and I slept better that night than I had in months.

After the move, there was a great deal of difficulty in setting boundaries with Rick. Even though we were still proceeding through the divorce, I desperately wanted to save my marriage, and tried to be as reasonable as I could.

This didn't always work because I was also trying to work through my anger at being betrayed and abandoned by an unfaithful spouse and being left to parent alone, again, and being alone, again. The cards I knew how to play were being angry and demanding my own way. Becoming more Christlike and aligning my behavior with the fruits of the Spirit was still new to me. Passionate emotions ruled my life as well as the actions and reactions that came along with them.

Once in the new townhouse, I vacillated between wanting to save my marriage, feeling obligated to save my marriage because I was a Christian, and wanting to move on with my life. The court process for the divorce continued for eighteen more months even though we really had nothing to fight about. My husband just wanted to fight. The situation seemed like a giant game to him.

Rick had told Pastor Waldo that he didn't believe in the Bible, that nothing written in Scripture was relevant to him. This brought into question whether Rick was actually a believer, and I was free to let go then and let the divorce proceed.

Pastor Waldo gave me three specific passages of Scripture to read through and memorize. I had read the Bible, but I had not really tried memorizing Scripture. The three chapters were Psalm 51, Psalm 139, and James 1. Psalm 51 helped me level set where I was with God, and had nothing to do with Rick, but everything to do with me.

The psalmist had written when he was repenting from the biggest moral failure of his life. David had come so far with God, was finally king, yet used this power to take another man's wife and have the man killed to cover it up. Psalm 51 helped me understand my own sinfulness.

Pastor Waldo advised me that in the marriage, I may only be 5 percent responsible, but I was 100 percent responsible for that 5 percent. This was a gentle way to get me off the pity train of being the injured spouse and take action. All I could see was my husband's faults and not my own. I couldn't do anything about my husband's wrongdoings, but I could work on myself.

Psalm 139 was also written by David. This Psalm talks about how precious a person is to God, what care God takes to know each one of us, and how He "hems us in behind and before." That God cared enough to hem me in amazed me, and I knew He would keep me within certain parameters while I figured out my life and this whole relationship with Him. Even though I didn't see the outcome, God did. Even though I didn't see the plan, God had one.

He knew me before I was born. He thinks about me all the time. He would guide me. I didn't know these things about God before. Certainly I had read Psalm 139 before, but had not understood the words like I did when memorizing them. This grew my faith and encouraged me to step out in faith.

The first chapter of James starts out by telling me to be happy about trials in my life. "Count it all joy" the second verse begins. I was not counting anything joy. I was counting things mad and unfair, and *Why is this happening to me?* But then I read that if I needed wisdom, all I had to do was ask God and He would give it to me. I did feel like I needed wisdom. I checked the verse again to see if there was a "to everyone but Robin" disclaimer. God would guide me, and if I was unsure, I could ask for wisdom.

Because my mom had shifted her expectations throughout my childhood, I was never sure which exact tasks I had to complete to win her favor. If you had asked me if God was like that, I would have answered no, but I would not have been able to give you an answer of how God actually is. But now I read in Scripture that God is steadfast in His expectations. If I didn't understand, He would help me figure it out. What a freeing paradigm shift in my battered thinking!

I revisited my earlier cultivated habits of listening to praise music and teaching when I had been in my sewing office. I began to memorize other Scriptures, many Psalms that were used as lyrics in contemporary praise music and solid teaching that encouraged me to search the Bible and learn more. For the first time in my life, I felt I really knew who God was.

Along with this new revelation from Scripture, I also reconnected with Todd to talk everything through. Everyone trying to grow needs a friend like Todd. He gave me three gifts that have been invaluable to me. Todd's first gift was his support, but he was a straight shooter because was not going to allow me to wallow. Well, maybe occasionally, but Todd saw the hard work that needed to happen for me to move toward maturity in my life and in my faith.

He set boundaries with me too. He had his own wife and family. Sometimes I called him daily, but if he had to go, he had to go. He was my friend, and he cared about me, but this did not make me the most important thing in his life. This alone was wonderful for me to experience because my personal business was not part of the evening news. It was not okay for me to demand that other people drop everything and help me handle my stuff. God is the only one who is always available to listen and the only one always equipped to help. Such a different pattern of thinking than I was accustomed to—and so much healthier.

The second gift that Todd gave me was the idea that my emotional "emergencies" were not emergencies. I could step back from the emotion and consider the situation before acting or reacting. The current of my emotions was in full control of my actions, but everything that happened in my life did not require an immediate action. I could set a boundary with myself for space to think situations through before responding. I could set a boundary with other people to give me at least twenty-four hours to respond. Once I started putting these boundaries in place, I realized very little required a direct response or action from me. I could let go of the feeling that I had to control all that.

The third gift that Todd gave me was the ability to sit back and logically think through a situation from start to finish without all the emotion. *How did we get here?* was just as important as *How we are going to move forward?* Many times I told Todd, "But I *feel* this way!"

Then we would go through the facts again. Sometimes I understood how the facts all worked together right away. Sometimes I had to think about the facts for a while before I understood. Sometimes I understood a year later. This new way of interacting in situations and with people and my newfound boundaries took time to puzzle through, like my knotted yarn from childhood crafting. I worked until this process of stepping back and considering the facts of situations transformed into a regular habit.

For example, there's a story about choosing between hopping over a puddle and walking around it. This puddle is a picture of your double-minded emotions not being congruent with how you feel and what you know is really best for you. Allowing your emotion to have control can lead you to hopping over the puddle, which gauges how much you can get away with and how much you are willing to risk. What are the odds you will clear the puddle unscathed? This depends on the size of the puddle, your ability at jumping, and what the fallout of failure is. Another choice is to walk around the puddle and avoid all additional drama. This is the benefit of stepping back and considering the necessity of your involvement with the puddle. Walking around the puddle to avoid a hot mess had never occurred to me.

In the years I spent working on setting healthy boundaries with Rick, these self-care and thinking skills were invaluable to me. I learned the court system, how to file my own motions, and how to protect us legally. For years we met at the police station for visitation rights with my son to avoid Rick's improper behavior when he would stop by my house.

At one point Rick tried to have me arrested for denying his visitation after he skipped visitation to go fishing with friends. Afterward we spent time in court-appointed counseling, which included mandatory parenting classes. These experiences took a toll on me, and I was wary and weary as I began to redefine which battles to fight. Everything did not need to be a huge battle. I could walk around the puddle. I had to learn to let things go and even worked with my children to redefine the importance of holidays so we could avoid unnecessary fights.

In taking complete accountability for my share, I had set unrealistic expectations for myself, for my marriage, and for Rick. I had learned these expectations from my parents and did not understand reasonable give and take in relationships at all. Expecting your spouse to be faithful, to parent with you, and to work things out are all reasonable expectations, but expecting your spouse to do these things your way or within your time frame and expecting your spouse to do things the "Christian" way when neither of you are really walking with the Lord are all unreasonable expectations. I needed time and counseling to fully understand my own unrealistic expectations.

Even years later, correcting my unrealistic expectations and letting go of the idols of having the "perfect" marriage and being the "perfect" woman of God is still a work in progress. Looking back, not having a spouse was *the best* situation for me because I had thought a marriage partner defined who I was; however, because I am single, God is my spouse. I knew definitively if something was "wrong" in the relationship that I did it or didn't do it. This forced me be more introspective about myself.

I learned to spend more time reading the Bible, worshipping, and in prayer. Though I didn't have a husband, I could pray for other marriages. I could invest in other relationships. Again, I have to say that I did not in any way do this perfectly. For many years I continued to be double-minded because I wanted God to work my plan into His plan.

I accepted dates with men with thoughts of "how to land this man" without even considering if this was a man I needed to be going out with in the first place. These men were not interested in a long-term relationship and were not interested in the faith aspect of my life. I hid my faith so that I could feel fulfilled instead of appreciating these men for the people they were.

This dating conundrum I put myself through stemmed from two lessons in how I was raised. The first, a man completes a woman as a human being, and the second, wishing where there was no hope. Henry Cloud defines this concept very well in chapter five of his book, *Necessary Endings*. He says a wish is something you want that has no basis in reality, and a hope is based upon some action (not talking) that you have seen. I thought I was hoping with these men when in reality, I was wishing.

Once I learned how to apply this healthy concept to my wishing, I mentioned Jesus on the first date. Bringing up Jesus and the importance of my faith in my life almost never led to a second date. I had met these men on Christian dating sites because there were no interested or eligible single men at church. I realized I was fishing for men from the wrong pond. (I still don't know where the pond is, but I'm very happy with my dog.)

Once I started teaching regularly at local community colleges and started small business consulting in addition to sewing costumes, my income stabilized, and I wasn't as concerned about the financial security of a boyfriend or a spouse. My emotional security was starting to firm up pretty well with Jesus.

8

Building a Dam

*I believe that I shall look upon the goodness of the LORD
in the land of the living! Wait for the LORD; be strong
and let your heart take courage; wait for the LORD!*
Psalm 27:1 ESV

THE GREATEST SOURCE OF restoration to the erosion of my personal landscape has repeatedly come through my children.
Something clicked inside me when I gave birth to Joey, my oldest
daughter. She was everything to me in a way I never realized could
be. I realized the moment I first held her the weight of the responsibility and the privilege of being her mother. I wanted everything
to be the very best for her, I wanted to be the very best for her, and
could envision her being intelligent and funny and beautiful and
strong, a woman of good character. She would be a credit to the
human race. I still felt this way when she colored on her bedroom

wall with crayons and stomped her feet when she didn't get her way. We were only a small-family unit, but we were a solid team.

My second daughter was born three years later. Easily overstimulated, she had her own way of doing life even as an infant. Juli was everything to me in a different way than her sister. I wanted everything to be the very best for her, and I wanted to be the very best for her. I could envision her being intelligent and funny and beautiful and strong, a woman of good character. She would be a credit to the human race. I still felt this way when she rolled her pacifier in the dirt and put it back in her mouth and when she ate carpenter ants because they tasted sweet. The three of us were a solid team.

Things were no different when I had my son six years later. He was my little boy and I was so happy to have a son in addition to my daughters. I identified with him the most because we were both the youngest. I was not as strict with him as I had been with the girls. I was more open to discussions and explanations. He did not understand things in the same way my girls did. I wanted everything to be the very best for him and wanted to be the very best mother for him. Though I had to learn different ways to parent with him, I could envision him being intelligent, funny, handsome and strong, a man of good character. He would be a credit to the human race. I still felt this way when he had difficulty in school because he would get the directions mixed up and when he struggled to sit still in class. The four of us were a solid team.

My children's need for me to be the best me I could be motivated me to pursue my faith, set good boundaries with myself, and set up good boundaries for them, protecting them from their sense of self-eroding. In areas where I recognized I had had no direction, I worked one step at a time to correct these for my children.

The impact of having had no frame of reference for directions really hit home when my daughter, Juli, was seven. We had an apartment with a dishwasher that didn't always fit all the dishes for a family of five. We had lasagna that night and there were a lot of dishes and pans.

"Mom, can I help you with the dishes?" Juli asked me after dinner.

"Sure!" I said. I was really proud of her willingness to help. "Help me clear the table and I'll show you how to load the dishwasher."

"Okay!" Juli brought all the dishes and pans from the table into the kitchen then climbed up on a footstool so she could reach all the way into the deep sink.

I showed Juli how to rinse the pans and dishes and load the dishwasher. But the dishwasher was partially filled from the pans used to prepare the meal. There wasn't enough room for all the plates, and I figured these would be easy for Juli to do by hand in the sink and leave to dry in the dish rack.

"The dishwasher is loaded, but these plates still need to be clean. Do you think you can do that?" I asked Juli.

"Sure, Mom. I can do it," Juli said confidently, taking the brush and starting on the first plate in the soapy water. I left the kitchen to leave her to the plates.

"I'm all done," Julie said, coming to get me fifteen minutes later. Come and see." The plates were placed just as she had seen me do, but the plates were only clean on the front. Lasagna grease covered the backs of the plates. We hadn't rinsed the backs of the plates for the dishwasher, so Juli didn't know how to do that.

As a parent, I had a choice in this moment. Juli was so proud of what she had done, and I wanted her to be willing to help in the future, but the dishes still needed to be cleaned. Quickly envisioning what the outcome would have been for me in this situation growing up, I realized I had walked away with the expectation that a seven-year-old would be able to dishes perfectly on the very first try.

"Hey, sweetie," I said. "You did such a good job putting the plates in the rack and look how nice the fronts look!" Juli beamed while I was talking. "The back of the plates need to be cleaned too, though."

"Oh, Mom." Juli sighed, and all the joy vanished. "I'm sorry."

"That's not your fault, Juli, and I'm sorry. I should have shown you how to do this instead of letting you do it alone. Let's finish these together."

The beam was back, and we finished the dishes together. In this situation, I chose not to pass on the standard of perfection to my daughter. I wish all of my parenting moments with Juli and my other children had turned out as well as this one did. One big win was realizing it before I said or did anything else with Juli. The other big win was finally being able to cut myself some slack for not knowing how to do things that hadn't been modeled for me.

Something else I realized about myself that hadn't been modeled for me was when Juli was eleven. Because we both have a similar build—tall with broad shoulders—we had soon towered over our peers in elementary school, and we had a couple of "ugly" years where our facial bones were moving into their permanent places.

But I hadn't realized how beautiful or intelligent I was. I didn't know how valuable I was. I grew up in church and had no idea how much God loved me or what Christ dying on the cross meant for my life. I saw the hope in the belief and embraced that hope but thought this was in salvation alone. God in his infinite grace is always working to restore what sin has destroyed in this life.

I had internalized all of this until one day, after a visit with my parents, Juli came to me.

"Mom, Oma told me I'm fat."

A tsunami of feelings from my adolescence flooded into my soul. All the worthlessness, hurt, feelings of inadequacy—all of it smacked me in the face.

"Yeah, she says things like that," I said evenly. The comment made me so angry because my mother was treating my daughter just the same as she had me. "She told me that when I was your age too. It's not true. You're growing and you need fuel. It's just the phase your body is in now. You're beautiful just the way you are. God thinks you're precious and so do I."

"Thanks, Mom. I love you."

"I love you too, sweetie. Don't listen to Oma when she says stuff like that."

Putting things in perspective for my daughter also started the process of putting things in perspective for myself. My mom's damage did not have to be Juli's damage, and it didn't have to be mine either. I had never considered healing from this abuse because I guess I didn't believe healing was possible. But in this situation, I saw this reversal with my daughter, and I began to think there were possibilities. For instance, I was able to stand up for my daughter in a way no one had stood up for me.

Redeeming holidays was a special source of peace and grounding for me. The Christmas my kids were fifteen, twelve, and six, we all went to my parents' for Christmas. My mother made a point of going out to lunch and then taking me shopping for clothes as a gift. My kids seemed so happy spending time with my father that I agreed.

We would shop at Lane Bryant because this was the store with a selection of clothes in my size. I had settled into a comfortable 22/24 at this point. I wasn't happy with the size, but this is where I was with my weight. I did not dress up for lunches anymore and hadn't for years. My matronly form was more inclined to long sweaters and stretch pants and what I wore to work and to "dress up." The rest of the time I was in sweatpants and a T-shirt or pajamas. I desperately wanted to lose weight and at the same time didn't want to care about my weight. The mountain of weight loss seemed so huge and unscalable because I needed to focus on single parenting and earning a living.

Mom and I went to a restaurant we had visited several times in my childhood. Only a few hearty plants decorated the lobby now, and there was no line of waiting people because instead of a hostess, a sign welcomed patrons to seat themselves. The once-fancy podium, now worn from use and time and minus the gilt lamp, had been pushed slightly to the side. The restaurant was now an average place with comforting but average food.

"Let's get a booth." My mother pointed to a section of booths in the middle of the restaurant.

I simply murmured in agreement. As we made our way to the booth, my mother glanced around at the other patrons but made no comments about their shoes or what they were wearing. Skylight ceilings still illuminated the decorated center with blooming flowers, though now there were more plants in between the colorful blooms. We settled into our booth and perused our menus.

"How is everything going with Joey?" my mother asked, folding her hands, looking at me directly as she had in lunches past. The conversation would immediately begin with my children from oldest to youngest. Eye contact during the conversation was imperative.

"Joey is doing great in school. She really enjoyed being in marching band again this fall."

"How is Juli doing in school?"

"Fine." Juli was not doing fine in school. Juli was trying for world-class social butterfly in school that year, as junior high had opened a whole new world of fun for her. My father would send the kids money based on their grades, and Juli had received very little money this time around. Whether or not my mother was aware of this, I was not going to subject Juli to any scrutiny.

"Hello, ladies," the pleasant-mannered, freckle-faced waitress in her forties said. "I see you found the menus. What can I get you to drink?"

"I'll have a water please, and a Diet Coke," I said.

"Diet Pepsi okay?"

"Oh, yes. Fine." I answered. "As long as it's diet and has caffeine, I'm good." I no longer wanted milkshakes with meals. Diet soda had replaced most of what I drank during the day.

"Please bring me a water and an iced tea," my mother said. "What are your specials today?"

"Very good, ma'am," said the waitress to my mother. "The special is the Monte Cristo sandwich, and the soup is Minestrone. Are you ready to order or do you need a few minutes?"

"I need a few more minutes to look at the menu," my mother answered.

"I'll be back with your drinks." The waitress smiled and walked away.

I wondered if she was a single mother too. I wondered if this job was the best she could do for her kids, or if she had to fight tooth and nail for child support, or if her mother was disappointed in the way her life had turned out.

"Robin, do you know what you want?" My mother glanced at her menu.

"I'll have the Rueben with fries and a side salad," I said confidently. Foregoing one serving of fries during "stress lunch" was not going to make a difference with my weight, but it would sure make a difference with my anxiety.

"Hmmm," my mother said. "I want to try their Minestrone soup, but the bowl is just too big for me. I wonder if they will just bring me a cup of soup instead. I'll ask the waitress."

I didn't respond, but looked around the restaurant, still taking in all the changes from years past.

"And how is Nathan?"

"He is adjusting to first grade. He seems to be doing okay." Nathan hadn't been diagnosed officially, but the school system had rated him as having pervasive developmental delay (PDD). Because of this, Nathan had an individualized education plan (IEP) which required meetings with the school for issues with behavior and learning. In addition, he was growing rapidly, already ten inches taller than his average peer, so of course, everyone thought he was older than he actually was.

Next came the career questions. "How is your teaching going?

How were your classes this fall?" "Career" is probably a generous word because my mother was only concerned with how much money I was making.

"Here are your drinks, ladies." The waitress placed all the drinks in the appropriate spots. "Are you ready to order?"

"You start," my mother said to me. "Give me one more minute."

"I'll have the Rueben with fries," I said, "and a side salad."

"Ranch okay?"

"Yes, on the side please."

"And for you, ma'am?" The waitress turned to my mother.

"I would like the Minestrone soup, but I'd like just a cup, not a bowl. Can you do that for me?"

"We do have a cup of soup and a half sandwich or side salad on the regular menu. Would you like that?"

"Oh, I didn't see that."

"Here, it's on the other side of where you are looking." The waitress directed her to the correct spot. "We have the turkey club, a BLT, Rueben, half burger, and peanut butter and jelly available for the half sandwiches."

"Oh, okay. Can I have half a Monte Cristo sandwich?" my mother asked.

"No, ma'am. The Monte Cristo is the special today. That sandwich is not available for this offering. We have the turkey club, a BLT, Rueben, half burger, and peanut butter and jelly available for the half sandwiches."

"Uh," my mother gasped in half disgust, half disappointment. "It shouldn't be *that* much trouble to cut one in half."

"Would you like a few more minutes to choose between the options available?" The waitress tried to keep my mother on track.

"I'll have the turkey club," my mother said, clearly disappointed. "But I would like very little mayonnaise on the sandwich."

"Yes, ma'am," the waitress said, writing it all down. "Thank you. I'll put your order in."

As she walked away, I wondered how she had managed my mother so well, if she had difficult customers all day long. She seemed to just let the stress roll off her back, and I admired her.

"The service here certainly isn't what it used to be," my mother huffed.

"I'm sure that was a management decision that she's just enforcing, Mom," I said, trying to bring reason into the conversation. Then, deflecting just in case, "My classes went well this fall. I had two sections of Western Humanities, one section of Introduction to Business, and one of Management. I had good students in all the classes. A few of them in more than one class."

"Such a variety of classes," my mother said. "With all that talent, are they going to give you a raise?"

And here the need for comfort food started. "Pay is based upon the union contract, Mom. I can't go in and negotiate a raise just for myself."

"If they valued you, you could. How many instructors can cover business and humanities?" She shook her head in disbelief. "When will they offer you a full-time position?"

"I would go for a full-time position in the business department but there hasn't been a posting in some time."

"If they valued you, they would make a position available for you," she said, as if I were missing some magic to make the college value me to this extent.

The scorpions from my childhood looked at me like, "Really, you wanna go again? You know you lose every single time." Scorpion sting one complete.

"Has Joey's father sent you any child support?" Mother asked. Round two.

"The court figured out all the back support and everything is being handled through them."

"What about Juli's father?"

"Canada has a different system than the US. I've been trying to work to get support updated, but navigating their system is not easy when you aren't in Canada. Just like getting divorced from someone in Canada is not easy and takes time." I was hoping the parallel of something she had actual firsthand knowledge of would bring her around.

"He should be paying more. Juli needs more." But no, the first-hand knowledge comparison failed.

I looked at the table, trying to collect my thoughts. This same old argument again. Scorpion sting two.

"And what about Nathan's dad? They should all pay more."

My mother had no idea how much effort fighting in court for child support was. Getting the support set up had taken months. Two of my children's fathers were in different states from where we lived, and one was in Canada. I had spent four years working through the court system getting child support for my eldest daughter adjusted while her father lived in another state. Four years of advocating, waiting, making phone calls, filing paperwork, filling out paperwork, talking to case workers, staying on case workers, working with the state's attorney's office, going to court, and taking time off from work.

Explaining all of this effort to my mother would result in her picking apart every piece. Like someone with zero experience fixing cars hovering over the mechanic to direct a transmission replacement who at some point obstructs the progress by the distraction, my mother would pick apart all of my effort without having a frame of reference: no firsthand knowledge of the process, no experience with doing it herself. Our "relationship" had shifted from my mother dictating who I was to become to now my mother dictating demands without understanding or caring who I was or the scope of the situation, simply because she wanted the situation to be different.

My shoulders slumped. I knew God was working things out for me and my kids, but I just couldn't explain this sufficiently to my mom. I didn't know how to articulate my faith to my mother, nor did I think doing so would be worth the effort. I saw the difference between what my mother was demanding and what God asked of me. God was willing to meet me right where I was and work with me to grow.

"His child support is also handled through the state. It's paid every month," I said evenly.

The waitress thankfully arrived with our food. "And here is some ketchup for your fries. Is there anything else I can get for you?"

"No, this looks great. Thank you," I said to the waitress. "Mom?"

"I think I have everything I need," my mother said, looking at the inside of her sandwich to gauge the mayonnaise level.

"Enjoy!" The waitress said, still smiling, and she walked away.

"So, Robin, I've been meaning to ask you about your weight," my mother began, taking a spoon to her cup of soup. This was the sign that the kid gloves were off. A more accurate statement would have been, "I want to know why you have not made any progress in losing weight," or "Why are you so fat?" Scorpion three poised for attack.

"There's a lot going on with the kids and work, Mom," I crunched into my salad. "Let's eat." I tried the same deflection my father used at family gatherings. It didn't work any better for me than it did for him.

"You reewee shud make um effort, Robin," she said while chewing a bite of her sandwich. "This sandwich is so dry, uhhh. You're rather overweight." She said this as if it should be some kind of epiphany to me.

I lived in my own body every single day. If anyone knew I needed to lose weight, it's me. "I'm busy with the kids and work. There isn't a lot of time for me. Losing weight is not as important as everything else I have going on." By now, I was tired of talking. There was no winning. I just wanted to stuff my face with my Rueben and go shopping.

"How about dating? Are you seeing anyone?"

I wanted to scream. "No," I reiterated. "I'm busy with the kids and work."

"Well, at your weight it probably is difficult to find anyone. Do you ever think about getting married again?" Stung by the third scorpion . . . twice.

"No." This was not true. I did think about getting married again. I thought about what it would be like to find a decent man. But I had three kids. He wouldn't just have to be good with my kids, a good provider, and good with my weight, but he would first have to be good with Jesus. Finding such a man seemed like another insurmountable mountain.

"You should think about getting married again. I would be so happy to see you happily married."

"I am happy, Mom." I was happy. The kids and I were a great team. Things weren't always easy, but they aren't for any family. The salad and the Rueben were now gone, and I was happily inhaling my fries.

Shopping was uneventful. Mom purchased some new sweaters and stretch pants for me as a Christmas gift. When we arrived back at my parents' house, I was still upset about the lunch conversation.

"What's wrong, Mom?" Joey asked. She and Juli were watching television in the library. Nathan was playing ping pong with my father in the basement.

"Lunch with Oma was stressful," I said. My girls knew what I meant. By now the girls had experienced enough of their own situations and were old enough to understand what I was talking about.

"Then why did you go to lunch?" Joey asked. This was a great question.

"It's part of coming here for the holidays," I answered. "If I'm here, lunch is expected."

"We don't have to come here for the holidays," Juli offered.

"Yeah, we don't have to come here," Joey agreed.

"We come here so you can spend time with Opa [my dad]," I said.

"We can spend time with Opa when they come to visit us," Joey said. "We don't need to come here for the holidays."

"Yeah, we aren't missing anything not coming here," Juli agreed.

This was the last Christmas we all spent with my parents.

Christmas was a tough holiday. There was still pressure from my mom to come back home for Christmas. I had to negotiate between two fathers for time over the holidays. The third father was not interested in any visitation. The whole time was very stressful. I was able to negotiate time between the kids and their dads for the same holidays every year. As a result, one year I would have all of my children present for Thanksgiving, and the next year I would have them for Christmas.

We scheduled Thanksgiving and Christmas whenever all four of us were home from visitation on the off years. Christmas might be celebrated closer to New Year's on the off years, but it was just as fun. This pattern of celebrations started some new traditions with our family. Each year we would invite people over for whenever our Christmas was and celebrate. I made pajamas for all the guests to wear. No formality necessary. Each year we would agree as a family on the food theme. One year we had Southern Christmas, complete with jambalaya, greens, and fried chicken. One year we each made homemade pizza. One year we had Chinese food Christmas. One year we had breakfast for Christmas.

My kids played video games or dominoes or cards in their pajamas all day in between eating and enjoying their presents. The four of us had so much fun with genuine joking around and laughing. With just my little family, there was no fighting over unrealistic expectations or stressing over meal preparation. We simply enjoyed each other as we created new traditions that were healing for all of us.

9

Planting Terraces of Grass

My God, my God, why have you forsaken me? Why are
you so far from saving me, so far from my cries of anguish?
My God, I cry out by day, but you do not answer, by
night, but I find no rest.
Psalm 22:1–2 ESV

IN THE BIBLE, DAVID lived with a bounty on his head while he
was in exile. I'm sure he found out right away who he could
really count on. His friendship with Jonathan was invaluable.
When I took in my sister-in-law, I felt I was in exile with my family, but I knew helping her was the right action to take. I couldn't
believe my mother was supporting my brother's behavior. This
action created a necessary separation between myself and my parents. I had removed myself from the unhealthy family dynamics
so that I could heal.

The spring after the last Christmas lunch with my mom, my brother and sister-in-law were having some difficulty in their marriage. My brother and Tracy had been married for fifteen years. My brother had taken up the habit of writing love letters to women in prison, and Tracy discovered the replies in the mailbox. My brother accused her of not trusting him and reading his mail illegally.

My mother refused to believe that he was doing anything wrong. After all, "men will be men." My sister-in-law and the church leadership disagreed. Marriage counseling started. My brother got better at hiding the replies. The counseling continued, and eventually the church leadership asked my brother to stop serving as an usher. Then, when the behavior continued after three years, they asked him to not come back to church until he could be faithful.

My brother was angry and told Tracy he needed some space to think about things. She stayed with a friend for the weekend and returned to find all of her things either outside or in the garage. My brother had changed the locks on the doors so she couldn't get into her own house.

Tracy called me in tears. "I just don't know what is happening. I did everything he asked." These words were so familiar, with my own experience during and after my divorce. There would be no winning, only the constant drum beat of demands. "I just don't know what to do. All of my things are here. I have nowhere to go," she cried on the phone.

"I'll come get you," I said. "I can get you a job in the neighborhood within walking distance. You can live with us until you get back on your feet." I drove to Michigan to pick her up and moved her into the ample basement of our Illinois townhouse.

My mother was furious. I had taken sides, the "wrong" side. Tracy had been part of our family for over fifteen years and now, through no fault of her own, she was the enemy? I couldn't set boundaries for myself, but I could set boundaries for Tracy.

"Gregg is wrong," I said. "He was wrong to write those letters.

He was wrong to change the locks on the house. He was wrong to put Tracy's stuff outside."

"Well, he's just hurting after all that's been done to him," my mother countered.

"Nothing has been done to him, Mom. He kicked Tracy out of the house because she wouldn't stand for his behavior. I can't believe you're supporting him in this."

"I can't believe you would turn your back on your own brother," she fumed. "And Tracy has spent all this money on credit cards since moving out."

"Tracy hasn't spent any money on credit cards, Mom. Tracy is living paycheck to paycheck in my basement. I'm pretty sure if those credit cards are also in Gregg's name, he's the one spending that money." I was so disgusted at my mother's stance.

"You don't have any proof Gregg is writing those letters. And that church mistreated him," my mother continued. Her argument was faltering, but still she persisted.

"Tracy is our family too." I maintained a calm tone. "She is welcome to stay here as long as she needs. I hope Gregg reconsiders and is willing to reconcile."

I don't remember the rest of the conversation with my mom, but I know that I had to end it. At this point I had had a lot of practice ending conversations before I lost my temper and then lost the argument. This resulted in me cutting many phone conversations with my mother short.

My father called me later to smooth things over. I had anticipated his call. "Rob, now how do you know that your brother is actually writing these love letters to women in prison?"

I was really disappointed in my dad and his lack of stance. The most guileless person you would ever meet, Tracy is the first to volunteer to help you in any way, to pray for you, to listen to you. She had done nothing wrong in this situation.

I was angry that this situation had been allowed to spiral to this point. Clearly my brother was in the wrong. I said, "That's a great question, Dad. But it's not the question you need to be asking yourself."

"Really, how's that? Enlighten me."

"See, here's the deal, Dad. Without Tracy to make sure the mortgage gets paid on time and Gregg feeling free to buy whatever he wants whenever he wants whether it's with cash or credit, it's only a matter of time before he loses the house. Once he loses the house, he'll move in with you and Mom. You know that, right? You know if he doesn't have a place to stay, he will live at your house. So the real question is whether you want to take the risk of having one of these inmates show up at your house, the new return address on the letters that Gregg writes, and steal your stuff, and maybe leave you or Mom with the crap beaten out of you. I hate to speak poorly of people I don't know, but these women went to prison for a reason."

"Robin, you always have an interesting perspective." This was the end of the conversation. We did not have the conversation again. My father saw the wisdom of our conversation and wasted no time making sure my brother's house was financially secure.

My brother called my house several times over the first couple months "just to talk" to me, but not to Tracy.

"Hey, Rob. I'm just calling to see how things are."

"Things are fine. Do you want to talk things out with Tracy?"

"No, I just called to talk to you."

On the third phone call, I stopped it. "I'm not interested in talking to you. You need to be interested in talking to your wife and working out your marriage. If you aren't calling to do that, then don't call here again."

Setting this boundary with my brother resulted in his never calling again. He told the rest of my family that I told him not to call my house anymore, conveniently leaving out the part about making the effort with his wife. My mother blamed me for the disintegration of my brother's marriage. There was a palatable layer of tension between my parents and me from this point forward, and I have not spoken to my brother since that phone call.

Tracy was understandably depressed. Her marriage was over. She was in her early fifties, living in a totally new situation, trying to make new connections. Tracy lived with us for nine months until she got her bearings and then moved into her own apartment. During the spring, she was issued divorce papers from my brother's attorney. After the divorce was final, Tracy said she did not want anything to do with my parents or my brother but was willing to talk to my sisters and me and my children.

The following winter, Tracy had some chest pains. I took her to the emergency room. The chest pains were actually a mild heart attack, which sent Tracy to the hospital for a quintuple bypass a couple days later. I don't remember how, but somehow my mother found out. She tried several times to contact Tracy through our church and through the hospital. Tracy let the church and the hospital know she was not interested in speaking to my mother.

My mother had asked me and my daughters repeatedly for Tracy's address. My sisters accused me of keeping reconciliation from happening because I would not facilitate connecting Tracy with my mother. There is a mistaken belief in my family that when you forgive someone, reconciliation happens automatically. But this is not true and certainly not realistic. Forgiveness does not mean automatic reconciliation. Reconciliation is not a "right" of the person who has been forgiven. My mother would not accept that someone would choose not to be in contact with her and was very angry with me.

But she asked in her most pleasant yet determined tone, "May I have Tracy's address and phone number? I would like to speak with her."

"No, Mom. Tracy is not interested in talking to you." I answered with a firmness set in stone. My sister-in-law was not interested in speaking to my mother. She asked specifically for me not to give her phone number and address to my mother.

"Well I need to speak to her," my mother insisted, the pleasantness from her tone quickly dissipating.

"She has asked me not to give you her address. If you want to send a letter to her, send it to my house and I will make sure Tracy gets it." I compromised.

Then I heard from my daughters that I was the reason my mother could not reconcile with Tracy. After eight years asking for Tracy's address, my mother finally did write a letter and send it, and as promised, I gave the letter to Tracy. There was no apology in the letter. There was no mention of seeking forgiveness or even any mention of wrongdoing. Only a few lines about how my mother missed her and that my parents used to call Tracy their "daughter-in-love."

Wisely, Tracy chose to not respond.

"I have not heard back from Tracy," my mother said. "Did you give her my note?"

"Yes, Mom," I answered. "I gave her the note."

"Well, she hasn't responded." I could tell from her tone that my mother did not believe I had even passed on the note to Tracy.

"I told you before that Tracy is not interested in speaking to you."

"Well, I don't understand why not."

There was no point in continuing the conversation. Reciting what my mother had done would only cause an argument. No change would come from the argument because Tracy would still not be interested in speaking to my mom. My mother's refusal to accept the situation was my mother's problem, not mine. A conversation with my mother would open a door. A door of permission that would result in my mother badgering Tracy until she agreed to make amends and resume their relationship. But the resumed relationship would be based upon my mother dictating the terms of the relationship, since no repentance or forgiveness would ever occur. The situation with Tracy showed me a large part of myself and how I could learn to set boundaries and continue to heal.

Another event that made a difference in my life was before Juli graduated high school. My parents came to stay for a week because the graduation coincided with my mother's high school reunion. Mom had self-published a book of fiction, a thinly disguised work of the first thirty-five years of her life, and had arranged to have a book signing at the reunion.

Beautiful spring weather that week sent my father and my daughter on a short walk where they saw a house for sale with an open house, and my father wanted to see the house. Looking at real estate was a common habit for my dad, as were discussions about where my parents would live or where I would live with my children. My father had had Parkinson's Disease for about fifteen years at this point. His mind was sharp, but his body didn't always cooperate. Upon exiting the open house, my daughter asked my father to wait so she could help him down the stairs. He did not wait, and in attempting to go down the front steps himself, he fell and injured his knee on the concrete.

I was giving an exam at the community college where I taught, and my daughter called me. I knew something was very wrong. Calling me in class for anything but an emergency was strictly forbidden. Briefly, she told me what had happened.

When I arrived home, my oldest daughter met me outside. "We got Opa upstairs. His knee is bad. He wouldn't let Oma call an ambulance and he wouldn't go to the hospital with Oma alone. He wanted to wait for you. Oma is screaming at everyone."

In the apartment, my two other children were sitting by my father whose knee had swollen to about three times its normal size. My mother sat stiffly in a chair near the door with her purse and lips clenched.

"Dad," I asked evenly, "are you ready to go to the emergency room?"

"Yeah," he replied flatly.

"Okay, guys," I said to my kids, "Let's get Opa down the stairs. Then I'll turn the van around." We proceeded to do just this, going slowly down the stairs. I went outside and turned the van around so the side door of the van, where the middle passenger seat offered plenty of room, could be right near the apartment building entrance. The effort required to get my dad into the van took all four of us, and throughout all this effort, my mother angrily fired off comments about how we weren't doing anything right.

"Are you coming with us to the emergency room?" I asked, in part to end the comments that still spewed.

"Of course I am coming!" she snapped. "I am his wife."

I kept silent for my dad. The goal was to get him to the hospital and have his knee treated, not to argue with my mother. No one else responded to her either.

The hospital was only a few miles away. On the way there, my mom talked nonstop about her book signing at her high school reunion that weekend. This was Friday and her reunion was Sunday.

Once at the emergency room, getting my dad out of the van was thankfully easier than getting him into the van. A security guard brought a wheelchair and helped me get him into it. My mom followed, and I went to park the van. I came in to find Dad in the hallway on a gurney with my mom standing beside him.

"Can you feel this?" she asked, repeatedly poking his swollen knee. My dad groaned in pain.

"Mom, stop that," I said, stunned that this was even happening. "You could make it worse. The doctor will see him in a minute."

"What do you know?" she spat at me. "You don't know anything. Everything you do is wrong. Everything you've ever tried has failed. You don't know anything."

The venom in her voice was palatable, like a needle jamming poison into my veins. If I responded in anger, it would only upset the situation further. I felt that I could not leave my father alone with her, that somehow his life depended on my staying and dealing with the venom.

She continued to talk to my father saying things like, "I bet you'll be back on your feet tomorrow so we can both go to the book signing," "I'm not cancelling the signing," and "Your knee doesn't look that bad."

I just listened while we waited, and when the emergency room staff came to take my dad for X-rays, I listened some more as my mom droned on with the same comments.

"Mrs. Vander Ven?" the nurse inquired.

"Yes. I'm Mrs. Vander Ven," my mom answered eagerly. "How soon will my husband be back on his feet?"

The nurse paused, schooling her features. Her tone was pleasant, but she couldn't hide her face. She was clearly surprised at the question. My mother didn't notice. "We've given your husband some pain relievers, and he will be back from X-ray shortly. The doctor will be with you in a few minutes as soon as he sees the X-rays. From the first glance, the doctor thinks the injury is not a break."

As the nurse walked away, my mother heaved a huge sigh of relief. "Good, then he should be up and walking for my book signing on Sunday."

"I need to use the restroom, Mom. I'll be right back," I said, excusing myself to follow after the nurse.

"Excuse me," I said. She was just around the corner. "You can't let my dad go out of here. My mom will force him to walk if he leaves the hospital. She will force him to walk on his knee unless he is admitted."

"I understand," the nurse said. "I will speak to the doctor."

"Thank you," I said.

My dad came back, having had his leg X-rayed shortly after.

Within a few more minutes, the doctor and the nurse came in to speak with my parents. "Hi, I'm Dr. Johansen. I've taken a look at your X-rays. I don't see a clear break, but with all the swelling, I can't say for certain there are no broken bones in your knee. The swelling will take three to five days to go down. You need to stay off the knee completely during this time and keep it iced and elevated. We'd like to admit you. Nurse Peters will take care of all the details."

My parents looked at each other. The doctor walked away, but the nurse stayed.

"My husband does not want to be admitted," my mother said firmly to the nurse.

"I don't want to be admitted," my father echoed obediently.

"I will go speak to the doctor," the nurse said calmly. I was relieved there might be some common sense injected into the situation.

She returned quickly. "The doctor says we can let you go if you take a walker with you."

"He doesn't need a walker," my mother said. "He can walk just fine if he tries hard enough."

"Here's the situation, ma'am. He can either take the walker or we can admit him," the nurse said.

"We'll take the walker," my dad said.

"Okay, I'll get that set up for you," replied the nurse. "The doctor recommends you cancel your plans for this weekend and go back home to Michigan."

"A walker?" my mother raged. "What will that cost? We are *not* going back to Michigan until I am ready."

I said, "Mom, you have good insurance. The insurance will cover the walker." My parents had retired with great benefits. There was no reasonable worry about coverage.

"Robin, there is a forty-dollar copay."

"Okay," I said. "I'll give you forty dollars to cover it."

She huffed. "You don't have any money. You'll never have any money. And this is why."

At this point, I just took the hit. I was thrilled Dad would be going home with a walker. Once my dad was released, the security guards helped him back into the van and we were on our way.

Back to my parents' hotel, my kids and I helped Dad back to the room and got him all set up with his knee iced and elevated.

"I don't understand why you need all this help. Why aren't you using the walker we just paid for?" my mother spat at my dad.

"Once you get home and the swelling goes down, I'm sure he'll still be using the walker, Mom" I said, adding an extra pillow behind Dad's back.

"Home? We're not going home until Monday. I have a book signing, and I need my husband to come with me."

"Mom, the doctor said Dad needs to be off his knee for three to five days for the swelling to go down. You're not going home?"

"No, we are *not* going home. I am not giving up my book signing. That is your interpretation of what the doctor said. And you," she said to my father, "you have ruined my weekend by doing this. I want my husband beside me and now I'm going to have to go all alone."

The kids and I agreed to take shifts at the hotel to help with my dad over the weekend. My mom went to her reunion and book signing by herself. She got lost on the way there and the way back. Me, my oldest daughter, and my son were with my dad when she returned Sunday evening.

My mother shoved the door open. "I stopped for directions twice and both these people lied to me about how to get back here."

"How did the reunion and the book signing go?" I asked, trying to deflect her anger.

"I sold two books," my mom said in a tone mixed with disgust and disappointment.

"Dad's all set," I said. "His knee is starting to look a little better. Joey has decided to travel back to Michigan with you tomorrow for a few days to help get Dad settled in. Dad has eaten. We're going back home to have supper and then I'll bring Joey back."

My kids exited the room to go to the lobby. Dad and I talked about the next steps of his recovery, how once they got home, things would be better than being in a hotel. He thanked me as I helped elevate his knee again after putting on more ice.

"You are going to help? You can't even help yourself! You have never amounted to anything. Nothing you have ever done has succeeded. You can't do anything for us."

I was stunned by her venom. The fact that my children and I had given up our entire weekend to help didn't matter. Nothing would ever be enough for her. She would ignore the directions from the doctor, and my father would let her. My father would choose to let her actions result in his death if this would satisfy her. But I did not have to make this choice for myself. I didn't have to let her kill me. I didn't have to drink the poison.

"Okay, Mom. I'll go then," I said calmly, putting the ice pack on my dad's knee.

"Rob, don't go," my dad pleaded. "I need your help!"

"No, Dad. Mom just said you don't. The kids are waiting. I've gotta go. I can't watch you let her do this."

And I left. I grieved for my dad and was sorry to let him go, but I could not be part of the madness any longer. The final scorpion had to die.

Until this point, I had attributed my family issues solely to my mother's behavior, but these actions from both of my parents completely disconnected me from the codependency I had been a part of my whole life. My dad was the "good guy," and my perception of enabling was that it only existed in families with issues with alcoholism and drug use, not families with anger issues. Enabling anger is just as destructive to relationships.

Fits of rage is listed in Galatians 5:20–21 along with drunkenness as a work of the flesh. Scripture calls believers to actively root out these behaviors and to lovingly support each other during the process. This isn't a matter of judgment but a matter of growth. Believers should be able to look at the past year, three years, five years, ten years, and see spiritual growth. This growth isn't a perfect trajectory and won't look the same for everyone, but this amount of growth reflects each believer's personal walk with God.

10

Planting Shrubs

*The LORD redeems the life of his servants; none of those
who take refuge in him will be condemned.*
Psalm 34:22 ESV

DURING THIS SAME TIME, I had struggled through several churches with various levels of spiritual abuse. Teaching at the college was also an abusive situation. My relationship with my mom was an abusive situation. Not healing from emotional abuse inclines you toward other situations of emotional abuse because these situations seem normal to you. Then, hopefully, when you get hurt, you realize the reality of the state of the relationship and choose to leave the situation and find a non-emotionally abusive relationship to replace it.

But maybe you don't realize it, and you keep clinging to the relationship because this type of relationship is all you know so this abuse seems normal to you. The unknown could be worse. Or maybe you don't think healthy relationships are possible for you.

No matter where you are or what situation you're in, God doesn't want anyone to remain in relationships that are harmful. God is looking for the best relationships for you and is continually working to restore what sin has destroyed. God is working so you can see his goodness in the land of the living. God is looking for your healing so His glory can shine through you as a bright beacon in this dark world.

There were two big issues I kept experiencing with church. People kept hurting me, and I kept depending on people to make my church experience work. The church we attended for nine years changed pastors. This was where my kids went to Awana and where I volunteered for years.

I wasn't feeling well and went to the emergency room. At the time, I had a high schooler and fifth grader at home. I had pulled a chin hair and the area where the hair had been kept swelling. The emergency room quickly identified the issue.

"Mrs. Meade, you have a MRSA infection. We need to put you in quarantine for thirty-six hours."

"What are you talking about? I can't stay here for thirty-six hours. I have kids at home and stuff to do." Self-care had never been my strong suit.

I called one of my girlfriends who was able to stay with the kids and accidentally scared my kids by telling them I loved them very much and was proud of them. The hospital rolled me into a single room and set me up with IV antibiotics.

My chin swelled even more overnight. I looked a little like an iguana. The doctor marked my neck with a Sharpie to chronicle the swelling, and the staff seemed a little detached, which filled me with anxiety.

In the morning, I called the college and asked for a substitute for my classes, then I called the church.

"Betsy, I'm in the hospital with a MRSA infection, quarantined for the next few days. I could use some help with the kids and the house. Would the church be able to help me?"

"Robin, you'll need to call your deaconess for help. I don't do any of this."

"I can do that. Who is my deaconess? Is it Marlene?"

"Yes, I think so. Let me know if you need anything else."

A little stunned, but too drugged to respond, I called Marlene. "Hi, Marlene. It's Robin. I'm in the hospital under quarantine with a MRSA infection. I just spoke with Betsy, and she said to speak with you about some help since you're my deaconess. My kids—"

"Robin, I'm not your deaconess. Ann is your deaconess. I don't know why Betsy asked you to call me."

I was a little stunned. "Okay, I'll call Ann. Do you have her number?"

"You don't have it?"

"No, I'm in quarantine in the hospital. I didn't think to grab the church directory on the way to the emergency room." I remember helping people in the hospital with meals or helping them with their kids. The situation seemed a little harder than it needed to be. I called Ann, but the call went to voicemail. I left a message and then I called Betsy again and told her the situation. "I thought you should know in case anyone else needs help."

"That's not right, Robin. Marlene is your deaconess, not Ann."

"Could I trouble you to call Marlene and work that out? I'm in the hospital with a MRSA infection and I'm limited with what I can do."

"I will call Marlene," Betsy said. "Oh, and Pastor Gary just arrived at the office. He says he's sorry you are in the hospital and will be praying for your recovery."

Our former pastor would have already tried to see me. "Thanks, Betsy." Tears welled up in my eyes. In between the calls, the doctor stopped by again and marked my swollen chin with the Sharpie. Was this it? Was I going to die from MRSA? I turned on the praise music playlist on my phone and just listened and prayed and cried.

The swelling kept marching down my throat. I didn't have any trouble breathing or eating but the infection was still progressing. The doctor stopped by and asked a bunch of questions about where I was and what I was doing. As if were in an episode of *House*. I talked through my day of activities that included teaching swimming. The doctor wondered if adding another antibiotic for a bacteria from pools would help.

Marlene called me back. "I guess I am your deaconess, Robin. I'll see what I can do to arrange help for you. I'm not sure what we can put together. But, since I have you on the phone, Karen Johnson is having back surgery in two weeks. May I put you down for a meal for their family while she recovers?"

"Sure, if I'm still alive," I said a little sarcastically. But I really didn't know if I would be alive. The whole situation was surreal, sideways.

"Great! I hope you feel better. I'll see what I can do."

This was the last I heard from Marlene, and I was disheartened and confused by Marlene's complete lack of caring for my situation.

The first evening in the hospital, one girlfriend stopped by with some clothes for me. My kids had cried in school that day because they were afraid something would happen to me. The swelling from the infection was all the way to the base of my neck. There was just me and God and the praise music on my phone. "My Heart Will Trust" by Hillsong played over and over while I kept praying, surrendering my future to God.

The additional antibiotic did the trick. The swelling started to go down overnight. I felt much better the next morning, and I was so thankful. My girlfriend brought the kids to see me that night. They just hugged me. I just hugged them. I was still hooked up to the IV for antibiotics, but the kid snuggles were the very best. My health kept improving, and two days later I was able to go home.

My girlfriends who helped me the best they could were not Christians. They did not attend church or want anything to do with church. After this experience, I questioned continuing to attend this church. When I got out of the hospital, there was no contact from anyone at church, and no one checked on me or my family. I had had volunteered there for nine years, gone to church with these people for years, and now I felt deserted.

I did talk with Marlene about her lack of help. "I told you I was in the hospital in quarantine with a MRSA infection and my family needed help," I said. "Why didn't you help us?"

"Sorry, I guess I messed up," she said. "You'll just need to forgive us and move on."

I decided to look for a new church home.

The next place was not much better. The leadership was misogynistic. Women needed to stay home with the children and be obedient to their husbands, and not question their leadership. Being a strong and independent woman did not fit in with this crowd.

Single moms can have it rough. There's a lot of assumptions people make based upon their own experience with single mothers or what they've heard. I was a single mom with three kids, the youngest had special needs. People in general have associated my son's autism as the cause for my being a single mother. Sadly, ignorance is everywhere, even in the church. Families that don't fit the mold are critiqued. No one from the church I grew up in would ever have critiqued my mother or father about the health of our family or about their parenting.

In all of my experiences, I've learned that everyone needs grace and we need to extend grace because there's a lot of mess from the sin in our lives. Especially in the church, we need to not make assumptions, but love people right where they are. That's what Jesus did.

11

Planting Trees

Investigate my life, O God, find out everything about me;
Cross-examine and test me, get a clear picture of what
I'm about; See for yourself whether I've done anything
wrong—then guide me on the road to eternal life.
Psalm 139:23–24 MSG

D AVID WAS ANOINTED TO be the next king of Israel. But before he became king, he had to wait for his promise to be realized. Even after he killed Goliath, a huge victory, you would think David would then be crowned king. He still had to wait for God's timing. Throughout my life I have also experienced this sense of waiting for God's promises to be realized in my life.

From a young age I have felt a strong pull toward something more from my relationship with God. Growing up, going to church was an empty exercise because I knew there was more, as if "more" was ethereal rather than tangible and designed for other people instead of me. Even though I caught glimpses of those tangible pieces, I could never reach them.

While raising three kids on my own, one child with special needs, I maintained a flexible schedule. Life was hectic and the budget was tight. While teaching business and humanities courses at community colleges and doing small business consulting, I also owned my own business sewing costumes for Renaissance fairs and historical reenactments.

The fairs were difficult to attend when my kids got older because my girls had interests other than helping me. I had considered they would need to explore their own interests when they grew up, but I had not considered how this would impact my sewing business. I sewed less, taught more, and ramped up the engagement with small business consulting. This change in work dynamic led me to volunteer more with the adjunct unions at the colleges where I taught because I was determined to make a difference for the other adjuncts.

Social justice seemed a worthwhile and godly cause. The adjuncts were being marginalized by the administration with little assistance from the sister unions on campus. Officer elections came and I won the position of secretary. This wasn't difficult since no one else wanted the job, yet I was proud to have won nonetheless and served with enthusiasm, creating a communications and marketing campaign to improve the adjunct presence on campus.

I set up a newsletter, and with help from Todd, set up and managed a website for our chapter. I attended our chapter monthly meetings and global chapter monthly meetings at the local union office. When our contract came up for negotiation, I had high hopes that the administration would see our value and be willing to negotiate in good faith. The result of hard work in the communications and marketing campaign was that I would be noticed and welcomed by the administration to "come into the fold." I ran for chapter president in the next election and won.

One of my board members warned me that I was being set up for a fall. The expectations that I had for other people were really what set me up for the fall. I have had expectations my whole life. I think this is normal because expectations are everywhere. The issue is when your expectations must exceed all other expectations. Because I had grown up where my mom's expectations always had to be met, I thought that my own assumptions as an adult would also be achieved. After all, I was putting forth my very best effort. However, those programmed but misguided assumptions and expectations flattened like a scorpion popping a balloon on the beach.

The politics in the administration and the union provided quite a challenge to these expectations. The contract was negotiated, but precious little changed for the adjuncts. I was no longer interested in having polite conversation to change opinions, so I wrote a letter to a board the college was seeking membership renewal with and laid out the mistreatment of the adjuncts. Within two days of the letter being sent, the college fired me.

Devastation overwhelmed me because I thought I was doing all of this for God. Social justice, making a difference, acting on my faith. Most of my friends at the college disappeared, and people were afraid to meet with me. The administration made it clear to the union that I would be arrested if I set foot on campus. But the college had clearly violated the Labor Board rules and my First Amendment rights. The union did agree to represent me for the case before the Labor Board, but I had to hire my own attorney for the First Amendment case.

I loved teaching as well as the opportunity to share knowledge, to see students have "aha" moments, and to influence people. But now I hated it. I didn't want to teach anymore. I was angry at teaching, angry that my service to these people didn't work out, angry because I couldn't see what God was doing. I was flat-out angry.

Looking for something that would bring satisfaction, I researched other options with small business consulting. Someone recommended looking into change management. The field of change management offered promise because the concepts of addressing the people side of change to ensure employee buy-in and user adoption of changes, were everything I had been employing in consulting, teaching, and volunteering. A beacon of hope. The challenge was my lack of connection with the corporate world. I became certified in change management and connected with groups and people on LinkedIn to break into this new career, all while making it with what teaching I had at other schools and sewing and small business consulting. Nothing was moving with finding a job in change management. My court cases with the Labor Board and for the violation of my First Amendment rights from being fired from the college weren't moving. Frustration soon mounted because I thought God wasn't acting on my behalf.

As I spent these months pouring over the book of Job, really searching myself, my motivations, and praying over Psalm 139:23–4, I laid my expectations for my union performance, my teaching, my parenting, my future at God's feet. I realized my motivations were good but they weren't what God had planned for me. If I wanted to step into God's plan, then I had to step away from making everything work on my own. I knew God promised to provide, and this was my prayer: "You promise for provision and I'm doing my best, but obviously I'm not doing what I should. Show me the path you want me to take, and I will leave all these efforts at making a living behind."

Within a week of praying that prayer, a friend connected me with a job where he worked. The IT project team needed help with the coordination and project management of a data center build being done within a corporate campus move. This was the opportunity I had been seeking, although I was really nervous. I had been working with project management concepts on a smaller scale— how would I measure up? Would they fire me after the six-month contract ended? The company was under no obligation to keep me.

I strive to pour my whole self into what I do, and because of my chaotic emotional upbringing, my first objective is to bring structure to whatever situation I am in. And this project needed structure. I reported to my friend who gave me direction on several areas where I could provide value to the team. The director and the managers on the project were complimentary of my efforts and kept giving me tasks to complete and areas to manage. I kept managing them. After we accomplished the data center build project, they assigned other projects to me. Six months turned in three years, still under contract. Three years of solid corporate experience in IT project management. Three years working with a supportive boss in a healthy work environment. Three years of cultivating new friendships and career connections and a certification in project management. A new career breaking forth, with God redeeming my past.

Even though I was working in the corporate space and creating new relationships, I was pretty much done with church and the relationships there. I had given up on finding a group of people to walk in faith with. There are layers to shutting down emotionally, and each layer can be so subtle that you might register something as "lost," but you can't articulate what it was. Like a fleeting glimpse of something perfect that instills hope as if it might be the cure for emotional cancer, it's gone.

Then I received a flier in the mail about New Life Brookfield, near where we lived. I told God I would give church one more shot, but if this one didn't work out, I was done. I struggled because I had been in church most of my life and understood that gathering of believers was not to be forsaken. I was good with God, but the leadership was so damaged in the churches I had been attending. In reality, I wasn't healed enough in my own life to set good boundaries, to depend on God instead of people, and to generously extend grace and forgiveness to other believers.

Because New Life's mission is, "Our purpose is to be a family of love that cooperates with God in making fully devoted fruitful followers of Christ," genuine love was first thing that overwhelmed me what I stepped inside. Everyone was friendly, smiling, welcoming. This wasn't the "happy, happy, joy, joy suffocating, we're all happy and you should be too" feeling that you sometimes get a whiff of when you enter a church service, but genuine brotherly love. The Greek word for this love in the New Testament is *phileo*, a feeling of friendship and shared goodwill. I was optimistic now. The worship was fulfilling, the sermons refreshing—but the love was the most important piece. The first service was such a positive experience.

The pastor and his wife, from my hometown in Michigan, were a real pleasure to speak with and so loving with a healthy, biblical outlook on life. I got to know other people at the church, and I wish I could say I came back every Sunday, but regular attendance took a while to work up to because trust had to be built. The love didn't stop flowing, and soon I was hooked. Within a year, I was teaching Bible study.

Through the volunteering and teaching at church, I developed safe, healthy friendships, different from the close friendships I had with nonbelievers because there's a special connection with believers who are working toward the same goal, becoming more Christlike. This doesn't mean the close friendships with nonbelievers are less, but these relationships did not address a piece of me that needed to heal in order to change and grow. I had never experienced this level of grace toward my faith walk in my friendships at a time when I was emotionally ready to work on my emotional healing. I could be my whole self here and didn't have to hide any piece from these people. They accepted me and I accepted them. We healed and grew together.

I started sharing my story of healing when leading Bible study. I was trying to create a safe place for anyone to share their story as well. Sharing worked! Other ladies began conversations about their tough relationship issues because they felt safe to honestly share and work on their chunks. Seeing the restoration process start in others made me realize my childhood story and healing process was not unique, as many others also experienced emotional abuse as children.

Following Scripture and working with a small group for healing can be done by anyone. I began leading and speaking at our women's retreats, and the positive response toward God by the participants started me thinking about writing this book. Seeing restoration in others' lives was an incredible blessing and provided me with further healing. There must be an emotionally healthy place for the layer to be well received. I had reached this healthy emotional state through my relationships at church.

Since I now had paid holidays, I decided I would go visit my mom. She mentioned she need help with a few things around the house, and I thought helping her was the right thing to do. But I was filled with anxiety because I had gained weight, and was already heavy when I started my IT project management job. (My boss brought in food for everyone to keep us working on the deadline, and not just sandwiches and chips, but very rich food from local restaurants. The food was delicious, and I enjoyed all of it.) Though I somewhat dreaded the visit because of my appearance, I committed to following through, and prepared myself mentally, prayed with friends from church, and drove to my doom.

My mom greeted me at the door with a big smile. "Robbie, it's so good to see you!" she said, giving me a hug. "Come on in. I have some tea on for us."

"It's good to see you too, Mom," I said, cautiously hopeful. She seemed to be in a good mood. This visit might go well. I followed her into the kitchen and sat down at the table.

"So tell me, how is your new job going? I was just telling Zelda at church how you have this new career and are doing so well," my mother said. "Do you remember Zelda?"

"Not really. I don't think I've ever met her."

"Oh, hmm. Well, I told her and my friend Corrine too. How is the new job going? How is your boss?"

"My boss is a great leader," I said. "He is genuinely concerned about all the people who are part of our team." Knowing everything that I said would be repeated, I was careful not to say anything specific.

"Let me pour you some tea. Would you like some sugar and cream?" she asked, pouring my tea.

"Sugar and cream would be great. Thank you," I said, waiting for the next question.

"Sounds like a nice man," she said. "I'm glad you're working for someone nice who appreciates you. Has he given you a raise?" The mountain scorpions stuck their heads and claws out.

"He certainly does appreciate me," I said. "He did give me a raise." Take that death blow, looming scorpion!

"Hmm," my mother said, very pleased. "Robbie, you look so thin. Have you lost weight?"

The remaining scorpions died spontaneously on site. I considered maybe my mother was suffering from dementia or poor eyesight, because I was at the highest weight I had ever been. But as I reflected on the conversation, I realized her focus was on the new career I had, and for the first time, I had met her expectations in both financial earnings and career clout—and because I had this new career, I looked thin to her. This drove home for me how arbitrary her opinions were.

The implications for me, however, were huge in this experience of finally being thin in my mom's eyes. My weight no longer mattered in my conversations or interactions with her. Similarly, my weight didn't matter to me anymore, and my focus changed to thinking about being healthy. What health goals did I have in the next five, ten, or twenty years? What would be important to me in these timeframes? What was important to me now? These questions mattered more because now I mattered more—not to my mom, but to myself. Holy smokes, I needed to get my act to-gether! I had plans to make! My damaged emotions still needed to be unraveled and the programmed habits and internal messaging still needed to be refreshed, but I was well on the path toward fierce wholeness.

12

Eroding No More

I will restore to you the years that the
swarming locusts have eaten . . .
Joel 2:25 ESV

Out of a sense of duty, I had agreed to another visit with my
mother for the day. Duty was truthfully not the only reason.
I had asked the ladies at my church to pray for me, to give me wisdom, and was hopeful that the visit would go well. I'm not sure I
could give you a picture of what "going well" would mean or even
look like, and one positive visit would not repair a lifetime of being
out of relationship. And yet this is one of my issues, always being
hopeful when there is no reason, always being hopeful because I
want the result to meet my expectation so very badly.

At the time of this particular visit, my father had been gone for
a few years. His death had shaken my mother in ways she did not
anticipate. The force of her anger was not able to prevent or delay

his death. She had absolutely no control over the timing. Her continual bickering about him ended when she realized he was gone. She repeatedly verbalized her regret for not appreciating him and how much he loved her over their sixty-three years of marriage. For a time, she was softer, more approachable, even though she continued to bludgeon with hurtful comments weighted by her expectations. She also used my dad's memory as a wildcard to get what she wanted: "Your father always did X for me," with the expectation that since I had been so close to my dad, I would follow suit and do X for her.

We were sitting at the breakfast table in the kitchen playing a game of Scrabble. Conversation had been fairly neutral. My trip up from Chicago had been uneventful. The weather was clear in Grand Rapids as we talked about the flowers in the front yard at her house and mine. She filled me in on all the news from her neighbors and her activities. She mentioned how my dad would have liked our visit, then asked when I would be able to visit again and stay overnight. I did not answer right away as I thought through the best response.

Then out of the blue, as she was bringing hot water for tea to the table, she said, "When I found out I was pregnant with you, I didn't want to have another baby, but your dad talked me into it." She stated this in the same manner as if she were talking about the day's weather forecast.

Stunned, I nodded for her to go on, politely. She kept talking, but I was no longer listening. What was she really saying? Outwardly, I made no move, lest I give my inner turmoil away and become an easy target. The familiar feeling of being in the wrong place, potentially saying the wrong thing, not knowing the "right" path, swept over me, and I was an adventurer walking through an old ruin, carefully stepping around known and unknown traps.

The statement flipped a switch in me, in the years of my healing process. All my experiences during my walk with God, my time in prayer, in Bible study, in searching for who I was in Christ, had led to this transformative moment. Before she said this, I had wanted to believe that she was changing. I was hopeful we could one day have a normal, healthy relationship, but I understood now that my close relationship with my father was a source of envy for her. Not because it was unhealthy but because the relationship threatened her absolute control. I understood that my father was trying to protect me, my life. He had not been able to stand up for himself, but to the extent that he could, he stood up for me.

What flipped the switch was what she did not say. She did not say that she regretted feeling that I should not have been born. She did not say this was why she rejected me. She did not say my father's affection for me made her jealous and that's why she took it out on me. She did not apologize for any of these things.

The things she did not say helped me realize how really messed up my mom was in her own head. Despite all she had been given, she had not put in the hard work to heal herself. Having faced and worked through the hard work of healing myself, I saw the whole situation now. Maybe she did not see the need for healing. Maybe she could not face the hard work of it. Either way, she would continue to cling to getting what she felt was due to her. She would not apologize and would continue to be who she had always been.

I, however, did not need to continue to be concerned about receiving any kind of affirmation from her. My affirmation would come from God. My affirmation needed to come from God and not any other. This was the answer to the tug I had felt my whole life. I was never alone. My value to God was never in question. This was the place where I needed to live fiercely with God.

On the drive back to Chicago, I prayed and searched myself and asked for wisdom with the now-familiar passage from James 1:5. Were my feelings of anger valid? Where was the line of respecting my parent? Was there any piece of me that needed correction in approaching this situation? Earlier in my faith walk, I had forgiven my mom after she hurt my daughter, hurt my sister-in-law, hurt my father, and hurt me. I hadn't understood the full scope of what she had done to me until now. In obedience to God, I forgave her so I could take a step of faith in trusting his sovereignty, to give myself some peace. This time I understood what had been stolen from me during my childhood and part of my adult life. This time, I understood all those unreasonable expectations my mom had for me, how she devalued my person as disposable, and how her rejection of me and any of my accomplishments was connected to this. This was the first time I could really let everything go, fully trusting God to make something of the situation. God had proven himself faithful in freeing me from the codependency that had chained me my whole life. Surely I could trust him with this situation as well. The freedom in letting go of everything was tremendous, like truly soaring on the wings of eagles and being completely restored.

People speak about forgiveness where a weight is lifted from them. This forgiveness of mine was a whole life's worth of weight, and I gained a fierce, whole piece of myself I had never owned before. My confidence was no longer rooted in my performance to please my mom, whose ideals shifted violently like the waters of a river after heavy rains. Now, my confidence was grounded fiercely and wholly upon who I was as a person in Christ.

Like David, I could repeat and memorize God's promises in the deepest place of my heart. God has gracefully given these promises to us in his word, so I can refer to them to double check when I am afraid or have doubts. These promises don't change. I know now that if I don't understand a biblical promise or what God expects on my end, I can ask God and he will faithfully grant me wisdom and discernment.

But unraveling all the hurt had to come first. Feeling secure in supportive relationships had to come first. Being able to be transparent about deep issues had to come first. Within our culture, we are accustomed to quick resolutions. Food is served quickly and delivered. We rely on pharmaceuticals for quick fixes or masking the core issue entirely. We self-medicate to deal with life *now*. We're all searching for the healing that God promises, without actually inviting God to be the center of our whole journey. This is the difference that God's presence makes. Lasting change comes from deep healing, and deep healing requires time.

My weight loss journey started with a close friend from church who faithfully prayed for me for several years. After the revelation visit with my mom, I went to the doctor to get a physical and my blood work done to know exactly where I was at in my health. The news wasn't great, but not surprising. My A1C was prediabetic and my cholesterol was way too high. My doctor recommended the keto diet. She had been researching the effects of sugar when on a diet, and for about two years, had been eating keto, even though she is a dedicated runner and has never struggled with her weight. As a doctor, if she were going to recommend a diet, she figured she had better be eating this way herself. I found this trait refreshing in the medical professional. She said not to worry about exercising at first, which I was totally on board with. I hate exercising.

Just to be clear, I am not recommending the keto diet. I'm just talking about my experience. Before getting into a diet, talk to your doctor. If you have been overweight for a chunk of your life or your whole life, you know that going to the doctor can be unnerving. I had a doctor who saw me for the first time ask when my gastric bypass will be scheduled. And I had come in because I had hit my head. Find a doctor who relates to you as a person.

I started eating keto after Thanksgiving. I tried different combinations of food to fit the 75 percent fat, 20 percent protein, and 5 percent carb mix to discover which recipes worked best for me. Once I began experimenting, I was amazed at the vast sources of carbs there were to consider. There were the obvious sources of bread, potatoes, and rice, but I had to give up bananas and oranges. I thought those were good for me, because they're certainly better than pancakes and potatoes, but they weren't keto friendly, so they had to go.

I was happy to find that foods with "good" fat that I love like black olives, sour cream, and crunchy almond butter could be included in my new food routine. My doctor recommended not drinking soda, which I pushed back on. I needed the caffeine. We compromised, and I agreed to drink one diet soda a day, but only with a meal. Within a few days of drinking the diet soda with one meal, I noticed the soda craving wasn't as intense as before. I skipped drinking diet soda for a few days and didn't get the usual horrible headache when I had tried to curb drinking diet soda. I realized I was addicted to the *sugar* in the diet soda, the way the sweetener tricked my body into thinking I had eaten when I hadn't. I stopped drinking diet soda entirely. I could handle this false craving by thinking through how I was feeling instead of giving in to an unhealthy craving. The only time I cheated from beginning the diet was on Christmas Day.

My first visit to the doctor was in January. I had lost seven pounds and four inches off my hips. Seven pounds and four inches from *just* eating keto—and not exercising!

"Seven pounds. That's good progress!" My doctor smiled, genuinely happy with my progress. This took a bit to sink in. Really? I thought I had lost at least ten, maybe even fifteen pounds. My head flooded with disappointment because my expectations had been higher.

We continued to discuss my progress. Because of the diet and losing seven pounds, I had quit drinking soda. Because of the diet and losing seven pounds, I felt more energized throughout the day. Because of the diet and losing seven pounds, I was more active, without tendon issues in my ankle stopping me completely. Because of the diet and losing seven pounds, I was sleeping better throughout the night. My doctor was so positive about all this progress, and here I was kicking myself over losing only seven pounds.

After leaving her office, I reflected on and analyzed our conversation. Originally I had wanted to lose seventy-five pounds. Yet in roughly six weeks, over the Christmas holiday season, without regular workouts, I had lost only seven pounds. This accomplished the first 10 percent of my goal. On top of this, I kicked a lifelong habit of drinking a substance with absolutely no nutritional or health benefit. My doctor had been pleased and positive with my progress, so why shouldn't I be? Maybe I was looking at the situation from the wrong perspective. I decided to be pleased with my progress.

But I wondered why this paradigm shift in my thinking had to happen in the first place. The answer revealed itself as the need to reset one more programmed pattern of thinking from my childhood. Progress had never been praised for the sake of encouragement but had been buried under a heap of critique and criticism, which resulted in perfectionism. And it is perfectionism that both pushes me toward goals and repels my ability to recognize or appreciate my own progress.

I decided to rest in the accomplishment of losing the seven pounds and continue the journey up the "becoming the healthiest me" mountain. One of the unhealthy relationship situations Henry Cloud defines is the "one up" relationship, in which one person in the relationship feels the need to have a position of superiority over another person in order to be in a relationship with them. In reality, this isn't really a relationship. In previous weight loss journeys, I found myself having this relationship with myself. In my own head, I was either putting myself down for lack of progress or having feelings of superiority toward others because of my progress. This form of pride cut me off from emotional healing. I either didn't feel worthy enough to discuss the situation with anyone, or I felt too far above anyone to discuss it. I would have a victory and be flooded with pride, which certainly deeply influenced my interactions with other people.

The weight loss continued, without exercise. Losing weight is only one part of setting boundaries with myself, of engaging actively in self-care. I started doing some research about body types and factors for weight loss. From this I realized stress is one of the key factors for not losing weight. Expecting myself to just keep going and handle everything is unrealistic and unhealthy. I love my career, but it is stressful. Projects deal with deadlines and setbacks. People involved in working on projects get stressed, and their less desirable personality traits surface, creating more stress. The contract I was working on lacked solid leadership and clear goals and involved a ton of stress with interpersonal relationships—not to mention long hours. Another job opportunity presented itself, and I decided to take it to reduce the amount of stress in my life.

The new position required me to be in the office, so I had to face dressing up and looking professional. Working from home at the other job had allowed me to wear my pajamas. My closet had plenty of professional clothes in different sizes. I topped out at a size twenty-four for dress slacks. (They looked so sloppy on me that I was happy to wear pajamas.) But now I had lost some weight. Hesitantly, I tried on the size twenty-two. They were loose! I tried on all the size 22s because fit varies so very much in larger sizes. Half of them were too loose. Bonus! Since I had lost weight and inches, these pants were now long enough to wear with heels without adjusting the bottom hem.

My fat is thickest around my hips, so I dared to try on a size twenty, and even though I could close the zipper, they were tight. Just because you can close the zipper doesn't mean you can actually sit in them. Into the closet they went. Maybe next month I would be able to wear them, or perhaps the month after. The point is I had confidence they would fit comfortably in the near future. Hope. Not a wish, but real hope. I would not be fat forever. Progress would continue. I didn't need to quantify, panic, or plan out the results. I could continue being faithful in what I was doing and not be anxious about progress.

From day to day, I noticed changes. Simple changes, like being comfortable using a regular size bathroom stall instead of a handicapped stall. Did I really feel handicapped? No. Maybe the desire for more room stemmed from being tall and fat instead of being fat. For me, being tall means feeling too big all the time. Things are designed for average heights and weights. I'm accustomed to

ducking and scrunching to make myself smaller for crowded door-
ways and seats on airplanes, trains, and cars, but being heavy com-
pounds that effort.

Another day-to-day milestone was being able to fasten the seat
belt in a regular airplane seat instead of asking for an extender belt.
I felt like a regular person, like I belonged on the airplane. After all,
I'm an adult and I bought an airplane ticket. Why shouldn't I feel
like I belong? Part of this feeling comes from growing up with feelings of not being good enough, not being included, being a "third"
wheel, and not good enough to be included with "regular" people.

All excited about my weight loss progress, I went through my
closet and purged all the clothes that no longer fit. Some of them
had only been in my possession for a few months. Three bags later,
I dropped those bags off at the Clothes and Shoes Box. If you have
ever experienced weight loss after amassing several sizes of clothes,
then you can understand how thrilled I was.

Then I went shopping, even though I was only 20 percent into
my weight loss goal. My weight was still significant and weird. I was
losing weight everywhere, and the donut roll around my hips was
still a donut roll. However, my excitement was not unfounded, and
I began to see the hourglass figure from my youth in the dressing
room mirror instead of the frumpy madam pear shape. I flipped
through the clothing racks, looking at the XLs and the size eighteen and twenty options. Satisfied, I purchased several new outfits.

My fat is a weird shape. I had surgery before my last pregnancy,
which made my donut kind of twisty. I put on more weight, lost
some, and put some more on and lost some, but always with a net
gain. If you are overweight, I don't need to tell you how very widely
sizes vary depending on where the garments are made. How very
frustrating and debilitating shopping can be, regardless of weight
loss. Finding the correct size is only one piece. Finding the correct
fit that also flatters can be a completely different-sized garment. My
donut roll had been with me as long as I could remember. Losing
the weight did not immediately equate with losing the weird shape,

despite seeing the hourglass figure begin to take shape or with standard sizes being a "good fit."

At this writing, I now fit into the clothes I imagined I would wear someday. In fact, some of them are rather loose. Wearing them, long desired, will not be possible in a month or two. These are my favorite things. I've been waiting a long time to be able to fit in these clothes. I've dreamed of wearing them proudly again, or for some of them, for the first time. Without realizing it, the opportunity to wear them is passing.

What will I do with this opportunity of losing this weight? Will I wear these clothes, or will I fret over how long I will be able to wear these clothes? Will I kick myself for spending so much time being attached to the me I envisioned being in these clothes?

As I continue to lose weight, who will I be in different-sized clothes? Will I be my whole self and not worry about my image? Can I finally get there in new clothes without being weighed down by expectations or image issues? This translates from my clothes, to my body, to my faith walk, to how I see my whole self. Holy smokes, this is the whole enchilada.

13

The Beauty of the Landscape

*Finally, brothers, whatever is true, whatever is honorable,
whatever is just, whatever is pure, whatever is lovely,
whatever is commendable, if there is any excellence, if there
is anything worthy of praise, think about these things.*
Philippians 4:8 (ESV)

THERE IS A VAST difference between excellence and perfection. Perfection is impossible to attain, and excellence is attained by consistent progress over time. I wish I could tell you that I've lost all the weight and kept it off, but the truth is I'm smack in the middle.

Some people might consider this as a hit against my credibility in writing this book. Truthfully, I don't think I'll ever arrive, as

I'm always striving toward excellence in everything that I do, my weight loss included. This is only part of my story. As I become healthier, there is more motivation to exercise, but my motivation is always a few steps from teetering on the edge. Self-discipline is a skill I lack, the battle I am fighting daily.

I know I am not the only one who struggles here. The struggle is real with exercise, housework, money, relationships, and carving out sufficient time to spend with God. Things I should do yet struggle to complete. I share this because I know I'm not the only one who has heard the droning whisper, "You're the only one who struggles with this. Look at all the other adults who have everything all together." Renewing my mind with Scripture helps to change my thinking, but I have to actually spend time reading, reflecting, praying over, and memorizing Scripture for this change to materialize. Just as exercise requires being intentional about getting it done, housework requires a routine, and managing money or any other resources requires planning, when self-discipline and follow through are put in place, a person has strength and support for whatever they are struggling with.

Being in the middle seems fair since I didn't gain all the weight in a short amount of time. Neither did my behavior patterns develop in a short time. The idea of finishing is abstract because there is no list of specific goals with dates and expectations. I'm just normal me, working to grow into a healthier me. I have really grown in some areas, and I'm only steps away from stumbling in others. Both are okay. The key is that I'm good with me. There's no beating myself up over the stumbles. I've accepted myself for who I am. The expectations from myself and others no longer hold me, which is exciting, liberating, and frightening. Exciting because this is the place I have wanted to be. Liberating because I'm here. Frightening because I own every bit of my progress. I've shaken off the chains of the expectations from my lonely upbringing and embraced responsibility for my life as an adult. The difference is that I am not alone.

God and I are walking together, and I have a loving, supportive network of church family and friends to walk with me.

There are boundaries you set with yourself. If, like me, you struggle in your head with your identity, you will likely struggle with setting personal boundaries. I have been working on this in my faith walk for nearly two decades. I see the progress when I look back, but I'm not where I want to be. As a child, when I messed up, I would say, "I should have done X instead." My father's simple reply was, "Don't 'should' on yourself." As long as you are walking and making progress, give yourself some grace. Set a firm boundary with those voices that would continue to berate and condemn you. If you mess up, ask God to forgive you. Then put what you need in place to help yourself in a similar future situation and move on. You may mess up in the same situation again. Maybe you need more accountability in place or maybe you need to avoid the circumstance altogether in the future. Just keep striving forward.

Letting go of the belief that my mom's will must be done was a long process. Over time I gained pieces of myself as I walked closer with God, who does not change. Compared to my upbringing, my faith walk provided me with firm boundaries for where I was and where I could go. I headed down a path of deep introspection as I sought to understand what my real motivations were for the emotional reactions I had for different circumstances. There are so many layers to this emotional healing process and God is so good, so gentle, and so faithful to work with you on each one. I couldn't even see all the layers to begin with and if I had been able to see them, I probably would have given up.

I was taught the person in control was the one who "wins." The truth is that God is the only one in control. We have seasons of responsibility and accountability, but we are never in control. We are stewards. This frightening and liberating idea was counterintuitive to me. I thought the reward for being in control meant you got whatever you wanted, whenever you wanted. So, I strove to be in control of my life, how I earned a living, my children, my friends, everything. On the surface that may not sound bad, but in practice this makes for a lot of unhappiness on many levels.

The positive side of being in control is that you get to make plans. Remember the schedule on my six-year-old bulletin board? Planning is for sure my thing. There is nothing wrong with planning, thinking the situation through, having back up plans and being prepared. The issue comes when I assume that my plan is the same as or better than God's plan. You might say, "That's ridiculous. How could anyone think their plan is the same as or better than God's plan?"

In my flesh, I would typically respond, "Hold this for me and watch how my plan is better." There's nothing wrong with planning, but desiring to be in control over God is being double-minded. We are telling God, "I got this," "I can do this myself without you," "I don't trust you to do what is best for me."

Maybe the plan is fabulous, but you're not ready for it to work. God took a lot of time to prepare me to have a great job and be financially secure. This happened when my daughters were grown and on their own, but my son was still at home. Why couldn't financial security have happened when Rick left me? I can't answer all of God's reasoning, but I know my human heart. Having financial security at that point would have been disaster because I would have made financial decisions with my emotions. I would not have been able to teach my children to be resourceful, because I would have felt a burden to provide them with everything I could afford. Money would have trapped another generation in my family.

I'm still working on progressing through not being in control. This is part of every relationship situation I have—part of me, and part of my nature, not only in my personal life, but in my professional life and spiritual life. God has given me the gift of being a great planner and following through. In fact, my plans have extra plans. There is nothing wrong with planning. But God isn't interested in my plans when they don't line up with His. I need to continually seek to align with God through his word and through prayer. At the end of the day, the outcome of any of my plans is up to God.

I don't understand why my mom is the way she is. I've forgiven her, although when new memories come up, I need to go through the forgiveness process again. For many years, there was quite a wall of anger surrounding me, keeping me from breaking through to God's love. Regardless of the process I've gone through, my relationship with my mom has not been restored, because my mom continues the same behavior patterns and they are still painful for me to be around. Each person is responsible for their own healing. I've taken ownership of mine.

In her song, "Generations," Sara Groves talks about choices we all make, choices to sin, choices to be "real" with recognizing our own sin. She sings fervently for peace to cover her great-great grandchildren. This is the peace I want for my children, my grandchildren, my great grandchildren, my great-great grandchildren. I've apologized to my children for what I couldn't provide them emotionally because I didn't have it myself.

The talents I do possess I can use to glorify my God, which means extending grace to others, including those closest to me. We do not battle against our own flesh and blood. My mom is not the enemy—she's just a person in my life. My mom was not able to give me what she did not have herself from her own childhood. My mom was used to keep me from understanding and using my gifts. I can only take responsibility for myself, my own actions, and my own healing. My mom needs to take responsibility for hers. I don't know her heart or the full extent of her hurts, real or imagined, but this doesn't mean that I need to open myself up to a full relationship with her while she continues hurtful behavior. What I do know is that God has made me fiercely whole in him, and I want to seek to always honor him and extend grace to others toward finding their own fierce wholeness.

Forceful

He used "forceful" to describe me
In one word, and I laughed and thought,
You should meet my mom.
And then I remembered my daughter,
In high school saying, "Have you met my
mom?"

In raising three children,
Alone,
Courageous, tenacious and fierce,
Shining brightly
As an advocate

In standing for fairness and equality and justice
Alone,
Courageous, tenacious and fierce,
Shining brightly
As an advocate.

Now my daughters, women of substance,
Courageous, tenacious, and fierce,
Shining brightly
Are and will be advocates of change,
Forces to be reckoned with.

And I think,
Thank God for my mom.
Thank you, Mom.

—Robin Meade 8/2/2015

FINDING WHOLENESS

Study Questions
and Journaling

*But let him ask in faith, with no doubting, for the one
who doubts is like a wave of the sea that is driven and
tossed by the wind. For that person must not suppose that
he will receive anything from the Lord; he is a double-
minded man, unstable in all his ways.*
James 1:6–8 ESV

Chapter 1—Growing Up in the Floodplain

1. What is the source of water in your floodplain? There should
   be one source. There may be smaller streams that feed into the
   waterway, contributing to erosion, but one main source. In order to understand and unravel all the waterways, journaling is

a helpful tool. Using your personal journal, write your answers in the format below. An example from my story is provided.

Event	When did this happen?	Who was involved?	What happened?	How did this event make you feel?	Has this situation been resolved?
Book	I was 6	Mom & Dad	Abilities dismissed	Worthless	No

2. For each event that has not been resolved, write out what you think would have to happen for the situation to be resolved. Write this out step by step. You may have to do this in waves as you pray over the event and process how you feel. There will probably be a flood of feelings when you are thinking about the events. Pray through your feelings and ask God for wisdom, then write out what you believe God is impressing on you that needs to happen for the situation to be resolved or managed. If you ask Him, He'll be with you each step of the way.

Prayer

Lord, thank You for always being there to listen to me and help me work through all the unresolved hurt in my life. Please give me wisdom as I work through these painful situations to know what actions I need to take to forgive and to work past the influence these situations still have on my life. Speak to me as I renew my mind with Your Word, to gain new understanding of the path of healing before me. Help me to trust You to guide me through this pain toward wholeness.

Chapter 2—An Increase in Confluence

1. Do you struggle with your weight? If not your weight, what do you struggle with?
2. What is your earliest memory of struggling with your eating or the struggle you mentioned in question one? Using your

personal journal, write your answers in the format below. An example from my story is provided.

Event	When did this happen?	Who was involved?	What happened?	How did this event make you feel?
Lunch	I was 8	Mom	Stuffing my face with food	Worthless

3. This search for wholeness all comes down to faith. Have you accepted Christ as your Savior? Do you trust in Him to walk through and provide the very best for you? For the next thirty days, pray through Psalm 51 and Psalm 139. Spend five minutes each day after you read in quiet reflection of what the words in these passages mean for you in your faith walk. You can focus on just one or two verses at a time. Come expecting to hear from God as you quiet your heart and listen for His voice. After reflection, write down in your journal what you hear from God.

Prayer

Lord, I thank You that You know me so well. I want to trust You with my healing, my life. Please come into my heart, Lord Jesus, and show me the way. Please show me how this struggle is related to the hurt in my life and how You are going before me to prepare this healing path toward wholeness. Help me understand how much You love me and how deeply I can heal through the love that You rain down on me. Help me trust You as we walk through this healing process.

Chapter 3—Abrasion

1. Over time, huge rocks carried by the river's flow wear down the riverbed. This is a picture of outside forces in our lives that pound against our personal landscape and sometimes from

within. This may be criticism from a parent, feelings of worthlessness or failure, and relentless teasing from siblings or classmates. What are your rocks? Using your personal journal, write your answers in the format below. An example from my story is provided.

Event	When did this happen?	Who was involved?	What happened?	How did this event make you feel?
Holiday fighting	I was 8	Family	Fight between my mom and sister	Sad

2. "How did this rock (event) make you feel?" is the most important column in the chart above. How often do you think about the rocks in your life? Write out Psalm 139:1–18. Using your personal journal, write down five things that God says about you. How does what God says about you compare to how each rock makes you feel?

Prayer

Lord, I thank You for knowing me in my inward places and having me hemmed in behind and before. Help me to see myself as You see me. Give me the grace to see these rocks for what they are and the strength to let them roll past me. Heal me where these rocks have worn down my heart and restore me as I walk with You as You have promised in Your Word.

Chapter 4—Gradient Erosion

1. Denial and gaslighting can be powerful influences, especially with a child who has no other frame of reference. Romans 12:2 tells us to not be conformed to the thinking of this world, but to renew our minds with God's Word. Do these surreal events still influence your thinking? Write the five things you wrote from exercise three in chapter 3 on a sticky note or in a text message to yourself. The next time you think about this event

and start feeling pain, read the verse and ask God to help you accept how He sees you over how you see yourself.

2. Understanding love is really important to your growth. Read 1 Corinthians 13:4–8. This is the love chapter. What in your thinking is unloving, either toward yourself or others? Write these ways of thinking down and compare them to the characteristics of love found in the passage. Make a plan to replace the current unloving behavior with a loving behavior to make this your new habit.

3. Forgiveness is also really important to your growth. Forgiveness is not about restoring the relationship. Forgiveness is about acknowledging the hurt and trusting God to work the situation out. This means you can close the door on the hurt and move on with your healing. If this situation is in the past, this is an easier process than if the situation is ongoing. Using the information you've journaled already, pray over your piece of forgiveness and forgive in conversation with God alone. Spend time with God to consider if a conversation with this person is needed and make a plan for that conversation.

Prayer

Father, thank You for Your Word that is sharp and able to help me discern the healing that I need. Help me to trust in You even though I cannot always see what You are doing. Help me to have faith that You are working all of these situations out for my good and Your glory. I give the memory of this event to You. Help me unravel how I feel and why. Help me forgive those involved in this event, including myself. Help me to be loving where I am unloving and to create new, healthy memories.

Chapter 5—Lateral Erosion

1. As mentioned before, the main source of water filling your floodplain likely has/had smaller waterways contributing to it.

In the questions for chapter 1, you identified the main source of water. In this exercise, identify the smaller waterways which have contributed to the condition of your personal landscape. These would be situations that cause a continual drain on your life, such as a person who has an unhealthy attachment to you or a situation where you are doing more than you need to. Using your personal journal, write your answers in the format below. An example from my story is provided.

Streams	How did this event make you feel?
Gaslighting	Like I didn't know what reality was

2. Pray about these situations. Jesus says His yoke is heavy, but His burden is light. This means that Jesus expects that He is the one who is carrying the burden for you. Are you letting Him, or are you asking Him for help only when all of your own strength is tapped?

3. Romans 2:12 talks about renewing our minds with God's Word. Colossians 3:1–17 talks about putting on the new self. Just like renewing your mind, putting on your new self is an intentional process. Using your journal, write out where you struggle with the traits listed in Colossians 3:8–9. Then write out the response of your new self from verses 12–14.

Prayer

Lord, thank You being there for me when I need help. I need help! Show me when I am handling situations in my own strength. Help me to come to You first in prayer instead of other people. Help me to trust that You are working even when I don't see it, to trust Your plan, that You love me and know what is best for me. Show me where I need to grow and practice putting on my new self. Give me the courage to face and accomplish this change in my walk with You.

Chapter 6—Comprehending the Actual Deposition

1. Figuring out where all this water is supposed to go and where it is not supposed to go is the beginning of setting boundaries. In unhealthy relationships, such as with a narcissist, relational ties are skewed so that there is no end to you and no beginning to me. Where are you supposed to be? Is there water flowing where it shouldn't?

2. Everyone has gifts given to them by God. What are your gifts? What is in your heart to do? Is it painting, teaching, leading, ministry? These gifts may be reflected in things like "I've always wanted to do when . . ." Are there dreams you have had that you've given up on? Use your journal to record the answers.

3. What are your goals? Where would you like to be emotionally, physically, and personally if anything was possible? Use your journal to record your answers.

Prayer

Lord, thank You for giving me gifts to use for Your glory. What are they? Show me, even things I may have forgotten in the hurt of my life experiences. Show me the next step in using these gifts. Help me to discern the opportunities You make available to next use these gifts and to know when I should step back. Give me courage to step out in faith to use the gifts You have given me.

Chapter 7—Improving Drainage

1. Is your plan for your life working? Do you trust in God to walk through and provide the very best for you? This doesn't mean that you don't plan. This means that you submit your plans in prayer before God. This means you do what you can while trusting God to open the doors for everything to work out for your best and God's glory. The way this looks in reality can vary widely from circumstance to circumstance.

Using your journal, write out your plan and then the answers to the questions below:

    a. Did I really pray about this plan?
    b. Why do I want this to happen?
    c. What is my goal with this plan?
    d. How does this fit into the bigger goals for where God is leading me?

2. Read Galatians 5:22–24. This passage is about the fruits of the Spirit. Along with renewing your mind and putting on your new self, you will see over time that you will grow in these fruits. Using your journal, write out each of the fruits of the Spirit. Which ones do you display regularly in your life? Which ones have you grown in over the past year? Which ones will you work on building over the next year?

3. Situations can be *scary*. Life is full of them. Are you panicking every time a situation comes up because you feel the weight of having to carry this situation all on your own? What is the gap in time between talking to God in prayer about the situation and reaching out to others? Five minutes? An hour? A day? Set a boundary with yourself and spend time in prayer and then quiet time expecting to hear from God before you involve others. You decide how much time. Use your journal to track the situation and how God answers.

Prayer

Lord, I have this plan for my life. Show me where this plan fits or doesn't fit in with the plans You have for me. I yield my will, my plan, to Your perfect timing as I grow in faith. My desire is for the fruits of the Spirit to grow in me as I use my gifts for You. I know growing in these fruits is Your will according to Your Word. Give me grace and guidance as I reflect on situations that are *scary* that come up as I walk in my life. I know that You are bigger than any scary situation and You already have a solution in the works. Help me to show growth in the fruits of the Spirit in these situations, to shine for You in this dark world.

Chapter 8—Building a Dam

1. Building a dam involves lessening the impact of the water on the land. We've already discussed what the main source and contributing sources of water are to the flooding of your landscape. Using your journal, write out where you need to set boundaries in the different areas of your life. For your personal life, this could be with yourself, your spouse or ex-spouse, parents, children, friends, or extended family. For work, this could be your occupation, coworkers, your boss, or outside associates. You could also set boundaries at church with attending the church, the pastor or leadership, or other church members. Maybe you need to stop associating with someone who drains your resources and has shown no action toward change. Maybe you need to stop volunteering with a group of people who tear others down. Maybe you need to set up new traditions to protect yourself and your children from hurtful family situations.

2. Setting boundaries is hard work and *scary*. Boundaries take time and practice and you will certainly make mistakes. Making these mistakes exposes you to risk—the risk of losing support, the risk of things getting worse than they are now, the risk of being cut off from relationships. These risks are frightening, but God says He doesn't give us a spirit of fear, but of power, love, and self-control. Using your journal, write out these verses to encourage you in facing these risks. (Matthew 14:29–31; Philippians 4:6–7; Ecclesiastes 11:1–6; John 14:27; 2 Timothy 1:7; Deuteronomy 31:8; Psalm 32:8.)

3. Do you attend a church where you are growing in your faith? You will need spiritual support—prayer and encouragement—

with this process. Where will this come from? Who can you count on to pray for you and challenge you or hold you accountable? Use your journal to record your thoughts.

Prayer

Lord, I want to heal and grow in my faith. I hold to Your promise that I will see Your goodness while I am in this life. This situation (go ahead and spell each situation out before God one by one when you pray), requires a boundary with myself and with (spell this out too). I think the boundary that needs to be in place is (spell this out too). I'm asking You for wisdom with this boundary, which I know You will grant to me generously according to Your promise. Give me the courage to set this boundary, the words to communicate this boundary, and protect me as I hold fast to the boundary. I know You are stronger than any fear or anxiety this situation will cause and that You already have a plan in place for the resolution, because I am hemmed in behind and before. Thank You for walking through this with me.

Chapter 9—Planting Terraces of Grass

1. Planting grass in terraces helps to readjust the landscape so that heavy rain can soak into the ground instead of creating runoff that erodes the land. These terraces are a picture of the first phase of boundaries. These are small steps toward new habits which will reinforce your boundaries. Using your journal, write out three new habits you can begin to reinforce your boundaries. This could be as simple as choosing not to talk with someone who doesn't help you grow or choosing to try new hobbies to replace activities that don't help you grow.

2. Keep track of your progress with these new habits in your journal too. This is a really big step in reinforcing healthier choices. Don't "should" on yourself. Just keep diligently working on them. Mark your progress weekly.

3. Expect to face some resistance to the changes you are trying to make. People do not like change, especially if this change causes them to look at themselves when they don't want to. In your journal, prepare a response ahead of time for these conversations. This does not need to be an explanation. You can simply respond with "No," "No thank you," or "Perhaps another time." What is a situation where you need to prepare a response?

Prayer

Lord, give me wisdom as I create and enforce these boundaries, these new habits. Please comfort me in the anxiety I feel and help me to trust what I know about love from Your Word. Help me to display the fruits of the Spirit as I set these boundaries—love, joy, peace, patience, goodness, kindness, gentleness, faithfulness and self-control—and not to show anger or try to hurt others with these boundaries. I want these boundaries to be what is best for me, not used to seek to control or dictate to others. Give me grace to admit when I set the boundary in an unloving way and to try again in a loving way.

Chapter 10—Planting Shrubs

1. Planting shrubs keeps the ground strong and resistant to erosion by avoiding foot traffic, someone walking where they should not be. Who is walking across your boundaries? Who is trampling across your boundaries?
2. Shrubs represent firmer boundary settings. For me, this involved choosing to severely limit my interactions with people in my family and choosing a new church. Using your journal, write out what boundaries you need to set for people who are disregarding the ones you currently have in place.
3. Other shrubs you may need to consider planting are rescheduling holidays or visits to see people you want to invest in and

avoiding people who keep you from growing. Using your journal, write out what new traditions you may need to put in place. Pray over these ideas as you make a plan for them.

Prayer

Lord, this whole boundary-setting thing is tough. I see some progress in one place and a lot of resistance in another. Give me the courage to set firmer, loving boundaries in places where I need to and make plans for new traditions where I need to. Guide me as I make these, giving me wisdom and peace. I trust You to provide faithfully for me as You always have.

Chapter 11—Planting Trees

1. Planting trees holds the soil in place, stabilizing it by providing shelter for the soil from wind and water to lessen the impact of erosion. These trees represent your dreams, what you've always wanted to accomplish. In the exercises from chapter 6, we talked about writing down dreams and goals and taking the next steps with our gifts. What is one dream that you wrote down? What are your next three steps in achieving this goal?

2. Pray about these next three steps with Psalm 139:23–24. My healing process has taken me twenty years. God has graciously granted me a ton of victory *in His timing.* No amount of my fabulous planning has accomplished what God has accomplished. My planning only provided preparation for myself and a direction to seek God out and ask after His promises. What do you need to release to God's timing?

3. In Joel 2:25, God promises to restore to you the years that sin has destroyed. This is a powerful promise and the picture of God always working to restore in our lives. The idea of salvation is beyond reckoning, but God also promises His goodness in this life. We aren't expected to plod along drudgingly until we die to experience God's promises. That's where I was for a

long time because I had lost hope. I lost hope because I was trying to do everything in my own strength. Using your journal, write down Joel 2:25 and pray over this verse, claiming this promise.

Prayer

Lord, thank You for Your promises that You give me in Your Word that I may take hold of them. This (name your dream) is my dream. I give this dream to You, Lord. I trust You with it entirely. I let go of all my expectations surrounding this dream and what I think should happen in my life because of it. Give me the courage to let You have it and to faithfully work it out. Help me to discern when to act in favor of this dream and when to continue trusting and walking with You in anticipation.

Chapter 12—Eroding No More

1. Reaching base level, the place where the flow of water cannot erode is a process. There is no end date to this process. We are in this process for all of this life. "Winning" is continuing to grow in faith year after year, pursuing excellence over perfection.
2. Read the book of Deuteronomy. This whole book is a chronicle and testimony of God's faithfulness to the Israelites. Moses was reminding them of what God had already done for them so they wouldn't forget when they reached a season of plenty in the Promised Land. We are forgetful. We can stagnate in our faith walk. We need reminders.
3. Your journal should have quite a bit of content at this point. Using what you already have written, begin to write your own book of Deuteronomy. How has God answered your prayers throughout your life? Throughout your journey through this book? What else can you trust Him to faithfully provide?

Prayer

Lord, help me to pursue excellence, things that are true, honorable, just, pure, lovely, commendable, and worthy of Your praise. As I write my own book of remembrance of what You have faithfully brought about in my life, I look forward to the healing that I know is coming in other areas. Show me Your ways, Lord, that I may walk closer with You. Show me how I can continue to use my healing for Your glory.

Chapter 13—The Beauty of the Landscape

1. What milestones have you reached in healing? Have you lost weight, started a new career, met someone special? How does this make you feel? How close are you still to God?

2. Are you still waiting to reach a milestone in your healing? Healing does take some time. What will you do while you are waiting? Where will your focus be? Is your goal the healing, the blessing, or walking closely with God? Using your book of Deuteronomy that you wrote in chapter 12, re-read what God has done for you already to help focus your hope. If your journey is still fresh, read the book of Deuteronomy in the Bible to help focus your hope. Note all the miracles God performed for the Israelites to keep His promises to them.

Prayer

Lord, thank You for all the healing I have experienced and will continue to experience as I walk with You. Keep me close to You during the victories and blessings of my life. May Your Spirit convict me when I begin to stray. I want to be close to You first regardless of the blessings You have given me. Keep me thankful and help me to use my blessings for Your glory and not my own gain. Help me to show love to others who struggle with their own sin issues, to help them to know You more.

Recommended Reading

The Bible

Changes that Heal by Henry Cloud

Emotionally Healthy Spirituality by Peter Scazzero

Necessary Endings by Henry Cloud

The Courage to Be Rich by Suze Orman

The Mom Factor by Henry Cloud and John Townsend

The Walk of Repentance by Steve Gallagher

Order Information

To order additional copies of this book, please visit
www.redemption-press.com.

Also available on Amazon.com and BarnesandNoble.com
Or by calling toll free 1-844-2REDEEM.

CPSIA information can be obtained
at www.ICGtesting.com
Printed in the USA
FSHW011446270320
68547FS